Praise for Counterfeit Gospels

Evangelicals are rightly asking today, what is the go
Trevin Wax in this wonderfully readable and irenic
showing us that the gospel announcement is trunc
gospel story and if the gospel is not fleshed out in c

> Thomas R. Schreiner
> James Buchanan Harrison Professor of Nu
> The Southern Baptist Theological Seminary

This book clarifies the message and mission of the church as much as any book in print today. It is rich in both insight and illustration, very thought-provoking and very readable. I can't imagine a more helpful description of, and prescription for, contemporary evangelicalism. Return to the gospel!

> J. D. Greear
> Pastor of The Summit Church, Raleigh, NC
> and author of *Breaking the Islam Code*

Perhaps the single greatest need in the contemporary church is for Christians to understand the gospel and its counterfeits. Our lost and broken world is desperate for such clarity. Trevin gives it to us with this clear and compelling book about the nature and implications of the greatest story ever told.

> Darrin Patrick
> Pastor of The Journey in Missouri and author of *Church Planter*

This book is a winsome, creative, and compelling analysis of the pitfalls of a non-gospel or less-than-gospel Christianity—and a description of a full-orbed gospel Christianity.

> Josh Moody
> Pastor of College Church, Wheaton, IL and author of *No Other Gospel*

The biblical gospel of the atoning death and glorious resurrection of Jesus saves. Counterfeit gospels that leave out the bloody cross and neglect the empty tomb damn. It really is that simple. Trevin Wax makes crystal-clear which one is true and which ones are false. Unfortunately, this book is a much-needed corrective in an age seduced and deceived by imitations of the real thing. Eternity hangs in the balance when it comes to the gospel. There is no margin for error.

> Daniel L. Akin
> President, Southeastern Baptist Theological Seminary

Trevin Wax has done the church an important service by exposing the subtle deceptions that have trapped countless people within the church. Few topics are more important than the gospel, and few books help us see what makes it uniquely challenging and powerful as well as this one.

> Matthew Lee Anderson
> Blogger at MereOrthodoxy.com and author of *Earthen Vessels*

"What is the gospel?" may seem an odd and perhaps unnecessary question. It's not. It is an essential question that needs more, not less, discussion today. In *Counterfeit Gospels*, Trevin Wax has provided an essential tool for churches serious about the gospel and its implications.

> Ed Stetzer
> Vice President of Research and Ministry Development,
> LifeWay Christian Resources

Trevin Wax has served the church by identifying and critiquing many false gospels that threaten to ensnare us. But this book does so much more. Wax helped me love the gospel of Jesus Christ more deeply, and I pray that God will do the same for you through this excellent work.

Collin Hansen
Editorial Director, the Gospel Coalition, and coauthor of
A God-Sized Vision: Revival Stories That Stretch and Stir

When the devil cannot get a church to explicitly deny the gospel, he pits one part of Scripture against another and then nudges the church to change the gospel's shape ever so slightly—to re-configure it, to re-interpret it, to re-shade it. But Wax calls the devil's bluff. His *Counterfeit Gospels* surveys the landscape of these subtle reconfigurations, affirms what's true in each of them, and then helps us to separate the real thing from the imitators. A very helpful and insightful work.

Jonathan Leeman
Editorial Director, 9Marks and author of *Reverberation*

In *Counterfeit Gospels*, Trevin Wax does a great job of showing the many ways we subtly counterfeit the gospel and why we do so. His diagnosis of six common counterfeits is fair, insightful, and helpful. Like a good gyroscope, his book helps keep us on the right path. But even more admirable than his keen evaluation is the way he lays out a full-orbed and robust view of the gospel that includes story, announcement, and community. If Christians and the church would just understand this, we would not be tempted by so many counterfeits and thus miss out on the real gospel. I hope *Counterfeit Gospels* gets a wide reading; its message is needed.

Jim Belcher
Author of *Deep Church*

In a world filled with "different" gospels Trevin Wax reminds us of the call to "guard the deposit" that is the true gospel of Jesus Christ. If you teach, preach, share, or believe in the gospel of Christ, then you should read this book. It will remind you to maintain the simplicity and clarity of the gospel message that has been entrusted to us. I was both challenged and encouraged.

Anthony Carter
Lead Pastor, East Point Church in Georgia, and author of *Glory Road*

My super-talented friend Trevin Wax joins a growing number of younger evangelicals who are calling the 21st century church away from moralism and back to the gospel. He rightly understands that the gospel doesn't simply ignite the Christian life, it's also the fuel that keeps Christians going and growing every day. Therefore, we must be clear on what the gospel is or else we will conk out. I pray that this excellent book will help you come to a better understanding of the length and breadth of the gospel so that you will be recaptured every day by the "God of great expenditure" who gave everything that we might possess all.

Tullian Tchividjian
Pastor, Coral Ridge Presbyterian Church in Fort Lauderdale,
and visiting professor of theology at Reformed Theological Seminary

As wrong food, however nice-tasting, can threaten bodily health, so defective gospels always threaten spiritual health. Wax offers a bracing, health-oriented review of current defective gospels in order to wean us off them. Here is good medicine for the church.

J. I. Packer
Board of Governors' Professor of Theology, Regent College

counterfeit
gospels

REDISCOVERING THE GOOD NEWS
IN A WORLD OF FALSE HOPE

trevin wax

MOODY PUBLISHERS
CHICAGO

All Scripture quotations, unless otherwise indicated, are taken from *The Holy Bible, English Standard Version*. Copyright © 2000, 2001 by Crossway Bibles, a division of Good News Publishers. Used by permission. All rights reserved.

Scripture taken from the *Holy Bible, New International Version*®. NIV®. Copyright © 1973, 1978, 1984 by International Bible Society. Used by permission of Zondervan. All rights reserved.

Scripture quotations marked NKJV are taken from the *New King James Version*. Copyright © 1982 by Thomas Nelson, Inc. Used by permission. All rights reserved.

Edited by Jim Vincent
Interior design: Smartt Guys design
Cover design and image: Kathryn Joachim

Library of Congress Cataloging-in-Publication Data
Wax, Trevin
 Counterfeit gospels : rediscovering the good news in a world of false hope
/ Trevin Wax.
   p. cm.
Includes bibliographical references.
ISBN 978-0-8024-2337-5
1. Christianity--Essence, genius, nature. 2. Jesus Christ--Person and offices. 3. Salvation--Christianity. 4. Bible. N.T. Gospels--Criticism, interpretation, etc. I. Title.
BT60.W38 2011
234--dc22

                    2010048993

Moody Publishers is committed to caring wisely for God's creation and uses recycled paper whenever possible. The paper in this book consists of 10 percent post-consumer waste.

We hope you enjoy this book from Moody Publishers. Our goal is to provide high-quality, thought-provoking books and products that connect truth to your real needs and challenges. For more information on other books and products written and produced from a biblical perspective, go to www.moodypublishers. com or write to:

Moody Publishers
820 N. LaSalle Boulevard
Chicago, IL 60610

1 3 5 7 9 10 8 6 4 2

Printed in the United States of America

For Timothy and Julia

contents

foreword

THIS past summer my wife, Lauren, and I had our kitchen re-modeled. We live in an older home, and our former kitchen was literally falling apart. The new design, however, is amazing. It created more space and flows better. (This is imperative when you have three small children!) As we moved back into the new kitchen, we realized we had more room than we had stuff. This was true specifically when it came to the drawers. We now have an entire drawer for silverware, one for baking utensils, one for knives, and one for cooking utensils.

Another drawer ended up being what we call the junk drawer. It has no real rules. Anything can go into it. Right now there are batteries, a random wire, a couple of paper clips, some pencils and pens, random receipts, and an action figure that belongs to my son. This drawer has some similarity, I believe, to what's going on with the gospel of Jesus Christ today. Let me explain.

I have been encouraged and emboldened by the number of

cries for "gospel-centered ministry" arising within evangelicalism. From books to blogs, conferences to DVDs, there is a movement back toward what the apostle Paul says is of "first importance" (1 Corinthians 15:3). I am not a fearful man and passionately believe that, when it comes to doctrine and theology, a slippery slope is just that—a gradual slide toward what is incorrect. I don't believe that slippery slopes are cliffs with 90-degree angles. I'm no fear-monger. Yet we do see throughout the pages of Scripture some genuine (and not so genuine) individuals preaching a false gospel and calling it *the* gospel.

My concern today is with gradual drift. I am afraid that if clarity isn't brought to this word, "gospel," then it will become like that drawer in my kitchen—an ambiguous thing, a word we can change the meaning of, like "cool" or "bad." Put simply, I'm concerned that we could take the word "gospel" and make it mean whatever we want it to mean.

That's why I am grateful for this book, *Counterfeit Gospels*, because it aims to make sure we are talking about the same thing when we talk about the gospel. Trevin Wax wants to be sure we are all on the same page—which is to say, God's page—and that we are talking about what He means when the gospel is mentioned in Scripture.

I pray that your time with this book would be accompanied by the Spirit's whisper, and that you might repent where you need to repent and be encouraged where you have faithfully proclaimed the Good News of Jesus Christ.

Matt Chandler
Lead Pastor, the Village Church

counterfeit gospels vs. the greatest news of all

MODERN society lives in an age of terror. Unstable nations build weapons of mass destruction. Islamic fascists plant bombs in New York's Times Square, blow up trains in Spain, and create chaos in English subways. The threat of a nuclear attack constantly lurks in the background of our consciousness.

Now imagine a quieter weapon of mass destruction, a weapon that, when unleashed, can do as much damage to a nation as explosive acts of war. Historically one of the great weapons of mass destruction is actually nothing more than a piece of paper: a counterfeit bill. The most dangerous threat to our way of life might be something as small and unnoticeable as a missing watermark on a twenty-dollar bill.

The Power of a Counterfeit

For more than two thousand years, countries have sought to destabilize their enemies by spreading counterfeit money. During the Civil War, northerners sought to undermine Southern morale and the basis of its slave-based economy by forging confederate currency. Jefferson Davis, president of the confederacy, told the Confederate Congress in 1862, "Soldiers of the invading armies are found supplied with large quantities of these forged notes as a means of despoiling the country people, by fraud, out of such portions of their property as armed violence may fail to reach."[1] In the Confederate Congress, one legislator testified: "Wherever their armies have invaded our country . . . these notes have been scattered! This is one of the most destructive blows made against our government. The aim and tendency is to destroy all faith in the currency of the country."[2] By creating mass confusion regarding the value of confederate money, the North helped speed the demise of the confederacy.

Just think of what would happen if counterfeit bills flooded America. There would be massive confusion. It would take millions of dollars to educate the populace in becoming experts at seeing the truth in order to spot the fakes. By imitating the genuine, the counterfeit money creates confusion and typically distorts the value of the real currency. The counterfeit works because it mimics the real deal so well that customers and businesses spread the fake money until even governments are affected.

The Counterfeit Threat

Today many dangers threaten the Christian church. A cultural shift has brought accusations against the church as being extreme or closed-minded, militant Islam has increased, birthrates have declined in countries that were once known as Christian, religious persecution continues, and among church leaders moral failings still persist.

Yet the greatest threat to Christianity may not be modern culture, blatant heresies, or the rise of Islam. If the seeds of destruction can come from the counterfeit, could it be such seeds are slowly being planted through the counterfeit gospels *within* the church? Could it be that we are unwittingly participating in "printing" the counterfeit gospel? What if we are manufacturing counterfeit currency by the way we think and speak about the gospel?

All Christians everywhere must realize that we are at war. Our battle is not "against flesh and blood, but against principalities, against powers . . . of this [present] age," Ephesians 6:12 (NKJV). Awareness of the battle can help alert us to counterfeit gospels that the Enemy wishes to spread into our churches, counterfeits that will destabilize us, confuse us, and cause us to lose confidence in the biblical gospel.

Christians and non-Christians are often drawn to counterfeit gospels. Even those of us who have walked with the Lord for many years may be inclined to accept cheap imitations of the truth. Why? Because they are easy. They cost us less. And they make us popular with people whose opinions matter to us.

Yet a counterfeit gospel will always leave our souls impoverished at just the point we should be enriched. Counterfeits leave our hearts and affections for God depleted at just the time we should be overflowing with passion to share the good news with others. Counterfeits are like candy. They may be pleasant to the taste, but they leave us spiritually malnourished.

In extreme cases, a counterfeit gospel may lead to heresy, a distortion of the biblical gospel so devastating it leads straight to hell. But in most cases, counterfeit gospels represent either a dilution of the truth or a truth that is out of proportion. There may still be enough of a saving message to reconcile us to God, but the watered-down version never satisfies our longings. Nor will it empower us for service or embolden our witness before a watching world.

The Threefold Crisis in the Church

We need the biblical gospel, but we too often settle for counterfeits. Just at the time we need to be renewed by the biblical gospel, proclaimed in all its glory and fullness, a crisis has developed that makes this renewal difficult. The crisis has three elements:

1. A Lack of Gospel Confidence

First, we have lost our faith in the power of the gospel to change a life. Evangelicals often argue about how best to package the gospel. Some say, "We need new methods and new gospel presentations. Look at the diversity in our culture. We need a specific, fine-tuned way for each subgroup to hear the good news!" Others respond, "Our old methods work just fine. Don't mess with what has worked in the past. The problem isn't that we need new ideas; it's that we're not doing what we used to!"

Ironically, people on both sides of the debate over methodology act as if the power is in the package, not the gospel itself. Old package or new, it's the content *inside* that brings salvation.

I fear we have lost our confidence in the gospel as the saving power of God. One reason we don't share the gospel very often is that we don't feel qualified. We think we'll get something wrong. We lack confidence—in ourselves and in the gospel. But the power of the gospel is not in us or our presentation. Only the Holy Spirit has the power to open a heart; strategies, methods, and presentations are merely tools.

The gospel itself is powerful and deserves our full confidence.

2. A Lack of Gospel Clarity

While some focus on how we package the gospel message, others are convinced we need to tweak the message itself. We are told we need a new gospel for a new day. Bigger. Better. Improved.

Recent discussion on the gospel has led to a distressing array of options regarding the good news of Christianity. For a couple of years now, I have been collecting "gospel definitions" on my blog. I understand that people answer the question, *What is the gospel?* in a variety of ways. On the one hand, I'm reminded that we can never fully plumb the depths of the truth of the gospel. On the other, I see massive confusion in evangelicalism as to what the gospel is and why it matters.

The gospel is the heart of the Christian faith. If someone asked you to give them the basic message of the gospel in a few minutes, what would you say? Do you know the content of the gospel well enough to be able to clearly articulate the center of our faith? Would the basic message of Christianity survive your conversation?

3. A Lack of Gospel Community

Devoid of gospel confidence and clarity, our churches have begun to lose their distinctiveness. Poll after poll shows that the majority of those who claim to be born-again Christians live in a way that is no different from unbelievers. Because we are no longer confident in the gospel and have lost clarity regarding its message, our churches are looking for other things to unite around: politics, worship style, social activism, etc.

Ask yourself, *What animates and excites me? What makes my heart beat quickly?* Does joining with the community of faith in celebration of the gospel of Jesus Christ bring joy to your heart and mind? Or is church attendance merely an obligation, while your mind and heart are excited by other, lesser joys? The church is always tempted to lose its focus on the gospel and unite around something else.

The Gospel As a Three-Legged Stool

So what is the gospel? And how can we avoid the counterfeits that would deceive us?

In recent years, I've been encouraged to see a new buzzword

in evangelical circles: "gospel-centered." Many who use this term are seeking to bring renewal to evangelical churches by re-centering our preaching, our fellowship, and our mission on the good news of Jesus Christ. If we are to be gospel-centered, how-ever, it is vitally important that we understand the good news we stand upon.

I propose the gospel is like a three-legged stool. Each leg of the stool is important to understanding the message.

The Gospel Story

First, there is the gospel *story*, the overarching grand narrative found in the Scriptures. The Bible tells us about God's creation of a good world that was tainted by the sin of Adam and Eve. God gave the law to reveal His holiness and our need for a perfect sac-rifice, which is provided by the death of Jesus Christ. This same Jesus will one day return to this earth to judge the living and the dead, and thus renew all things. The gospel story is the scriptural narrative that takes us from creation to new creation, climaxing with the death and resurrection of Jesus.

The Gospel Announcement

The second leg of the stool is the gospel *announcement*, namely that God—in the person of Jesus Christ—lived a perfect life in our place, bore the penalty for our sin through His death on the cross, was raised from the dead to launch God's new creation, and is now exalted as Lord of the world. The announcement cen-ters upon Jesus and what He has done to reconcile us to God. Our response to this announcement is to repent of our sins and put our trust in the work He has accomplished on our behalf.

The Gospel Community

The third leg of the stool is the gospel *community*. Our response to the gospel announcement—repentance and faith—is not a one-time event. It's a lifelong expression of gratitude that wells up from the bottom of our hearts and overflows into love for God and His beloved community. We are shaped by the gospel into the kind of people who herald the grace of God and spread the news of Jesus Christ. God has commissioned the church to be the community that embodies the message of the gospel. Through our corporate life together, we "obey the gospel" by living according to the truth of the message that Jesus Christ is our Savior and the Lord of the world.

The Three-Legged Stool and the Counterfeits

Each leg of the stool is important because each relates to the other two. The gospel *story* provides the biblical narrative necessary for us to understand the nature of the gospel *announcement*. Likewise, the gospel *announcement* births the gospel *community* that centers its common life upon the transformative truth of Jesus Christ. Though the New Testament authors generally use the word "gospel" when referring to the announcement of the crucified and risen King Jesus, a closer look reveals that they never separate this announcement from the backstory that gives it meaning—nor the community that the announcement births.

So the gospel is like a three-legged stool. Cut off one of these legs, and the whole thing tips over.

The counterfeit gospels in the church today resemble the biblical gospel in some ways, and yet fail to incorporate and integrate all that the Bible says about the good news. Each counterfeit is like a colony of termites, eating away at one of the legs of the stool and therefore toppling the stool and damaging the other components as well.

In the chapters that follow, we will look in more detail at the three-legged stool: the gospel story, the gospel announcement, and the gospel community. We will also evaluate six common counterfeits that fail to do justice to the biblical portrait.

Each counterfeit focuses on one leg of the stool. For example, the first two counterfeits change the gospel story by either redefining the nature of the fall (therapeutic) or denying the judgment that accompanies the final restoration (judgmentless). The next two—the moralistic and quietist gospels—change the gospel announcement of Christ's work into good advice (in the first instance) or a private message of personal experience (in the second). The final two counterfeits target the gospel community either by uniting the church around something other than the cross (the activist gospel) or neglecting the importance of the church altogether (the churchless gospel). These counterfeits may look different, but the result is always the same. They leave us impoverished rather than empowered for ministry.

Join me with an open mind. Be ready to spot the counterfeits that creep into your own heart and lead you away from the glorious message of Christianity. Let's relish the biblical gospel together and determine to accept no substitutes!

Scripture Truths

The best way to recognize the genuine and the counterfeit is to look through the lens of the Scriptures. "Scripture Truths" will give you time to reflect on the warnings, encouragements, and teachings of the Bible. Here are several truths about the nature and outcome of the gospel.

THE DANGER OF FALSE GOSPELS WITHIN THE CHURCH: *Galatians 1:6–10; John 4:1–6; Jude 1–4; 1 Revelation 2:12–17*

CONFIDENCE IN THE POWER OF THE GOSPEL: *Acts 16:11–15; Romans 1:16–17; 1 Corinthians 1:18–2:5; Colossians 1:3–14*

CLARITY IN UNDERSTANDING THE GOSPEL: *Isaiah 52:7; Mark 1:14–15; Acts 2:22–36, 3:12–21, 10:34–43, 13:23:39; Romans 1:1–4; 1 Corinthians 15:1–6; 2 Timothy 2:8*

COMMUNITY BIRTHED BY THE GOSPEL: *Ephesians 1:15–23, 2:11–22; 1 Corinthians 12:12–31; Colossians 3:1–17*

PART 1

STORY

The Truth
the gospel story

A Counterfeit
the therapeutic gospel

A Counterfeit
the judgmentless gospel

I wonder what sort of a tale we've fallen into?

– Sam to Frodo in *The Fellowship of the Ring*

the gospel story

HOW MUCH would you pay to be written into a famous novel?
That was the question posed a few years ago by a nonprofit organization called the First Amendment Project, which hosted
a very unusual fundraiser on eBay. The Internet auction offered the highest bidder the chance to be written into the next
Stephen King novel. Seventy-six bids came in. The winner paid
$25,100 to receive literary immortality by, ironically, being killed
off in King's story. Other authors decided to help as well, including John Grisham, who promised to write the highest bidder
($12,100) into one of his books.[1]

It's amazing to think that people would pay big money to be
written into a famous story. Perhaps it reflects a longing deep in
our hearts, a longing to find our place in a story bigger and better
than our own personal story.

From the time we can put together syllables and comprehend
what other people are saying, we are fascinated by stories. Chil-

dren love fairy tales at bedtime, even if they are the same adventures they have heard dozens of times. Teenagers flock to the local movie theater to experience the latest stories coming out of Hollywood. Even adults enter the world of stories, curling up on the sofa with a good book, whether a biography of some famous person, a fictional drama, a romantic fling, or the history of a nation. From kindergarten on, we *live for* stories. Something deep within the human soul hungers for narratives and the truths they convey.

But stories are not merely for our relaxation and entertainment. We do not only live *for* stories; we live *by* them also. How we understand the story of our world affects how we live.

The Bible is a library of books that contain many different types of literature. Taken as a whole, the Scriptures provide us with a grand narrative—a great story in which every person is invited to take part. God has chosen, through His Word, to tell His children *the* Story, not a bedtime story that rocks us into a gentle sleep, but the story that we wake up to in the morning that explains why we exist. God's Story tells us who we are, what has gone wrong with the world, what God has done to redeem and restore His broken creation, and what the future holds for His people, those who accept His offer of salvation.

The fundamental questions that define our existence find their answers in the biblical narrative. And if we are to live *by* the biblical story, it's important that we rightly understand it and the good news at its heart.

Gospel Debates

As I have posted various definitions of "the gospel" on my blog, I have noticed that people hear the question "What is the gospel?" in different ways. Some hear this question and immediately think about how to present the gospel to an unbeliever. Their presentation usually begins with God as a holy and righteous judge. Then we hear about man's desperate plight apart from God and how our sinfulness deserves His wrath. But the good news is that Christ has come to live an obedient life and die in our place. We are then called to repent of our sins and trust in Christ.

Others hear, "What is the gospel?" and think quite specifically about the announcement of Jesus. They focus on Jesus' life, death, and resurrection. The gospel, according to this second group, is telling people who Jesus is and what He has done.

Still others hear the word "gospel" and think of the whole good news of Christianity, how God has acted in Christ to bring redemption to a fallen world. They focus on the grand sweep of the Bible's storyline and how Jesus comes to reverse the curse and make all things new.

Though there is significant overlap among these groups, advocates of each position often discuss and debate the others, convinced that taking a different approach messes up the gospel.

The Story crowd says, "If you only focus on the announcement of Jesus, you leave out the reason we need good news."

The Announcement crowd says, "You're adding too much to the gospel, confusing the truth about our sin or our necessary response of repentance with the good news itself, which is only about Jesus."

The New Creation crowd says, "If you only focus on individual salvation, you leave out the cosmic sweep of what God is doing."

The debate can be frustrating because the groups tend to talk over one another. But for the most part, I am encouraged by these discussions. Christians—young and old—are seeking clarity on the message that is at the heart of our faith. The motivation behind these debates is to get the message right.

The Heart of the Gospel

Having perused these gospel definitions carefully and followed the debates that surround them, I am convinced that the different approaches to "the gospel" are more complementary than contradictory. Of course, there is only *one* gospel. At its core, that gospel is the specific announcement about what God has done through the life, death, and resurrection of Jesus to bring about our salvation. The announcement of Jesus is the gospel.

Yet this Jesus-centered message needs context. The Story group is right to insist that the story is needed if the gospel announcement is to make sense. And the New Creation crowd is right to insist that we place our individual salvation within the bigger picture of God's glory in the renewal of all things. This discussion brings us back to the threefold sense of the gospel I explained in the introduction.

The gospel is a three-legged stool. There is an overarching *story*, which recounts our history from first creation to new creation and demonstrates how God will be magnified as our all in all. Then there is an *announcement* about Jesus Christ—His obedient life, His substitutionary death for sinners, and His resurrection and exaltation as king of the world. This announcement finds meaning within the story. The announcement elicits a response (repentance and faith) that then births the gospel *community*, the church that puts on display the gospel announcement by holy living that provides a foretaste of heaven here on earth.

As we will see shortly, each of the counterfeit gospels harms one of the legs on the stool, which eventually leads to the toppling of the entire stool. So it is important that we think clearly about these three aspects of the gospel.

Biblical Hints of the Gospel as Story

One of the clearest definitions of the gospel in the Bible comes from 1 Corinthians 15:1–4. Paul says:

> Now I would remind you, brothers, of the gospel I preached to you, which you received, in which you stand, and by which you are being saved, if you hold fast to the word I preached to

you—unless you believed in vain. For I delivered to you as of first importance what I also received: that Christ died for our sins in accordance with the Scriptures, that he was buried, that he was raised on the third day in accordance with the Scriptures.

On the surface, it seems that Paul is speaking of the gospel in terms of the announcement: Jesus Christ died for our sins, was buried, and has been raised from the dead. If the "gospel announcement" group is looking for ammo, they can add this passage to their arsenal.

But on closer inspection, we see that more is going on here. Paul repeats a phrase: "in accordance with the Scriptures." Paul is linking the announcement of Christ's death and resurrection to the promises made in the Old Testament Scriptures. The announcement is not divorced from the story. Rather, the announcement finds its meaning and fulfillment *according to the Scriptures.*

Paul is not the only New Testament writer who thinks this way. Each of the four Gospels also begins with a summary and recapitulation of Old Testament truth.

Matthew kicks things off with a genealogy, a long list of names that causes our eyes to glaze over. But just because we modern readers don't understand the point of genealogies doesn't mean Matthew didn't. The ancestral line of Jesus that Matthew places at the start of his Gospel links Jesus to David and then back to Abraham. The point? Jesus doesn't simply appear out of the blue. He is the faithful Israelite and the promised king through David's line.

Mark's Gospel is the shortest. He skips the story of Jesus' birth entirely. No manger scene. No angelic chorus for the shepherds. No star in the east for the wise men. Nevertheless, Mark grounds his Gospel in the Old Testament. He starts by quoting from Isaiah the prophet (who had much to say about "good news," by the way). "As it is written" is Mark's way of saying, "according to the Scriptures." So Mark joins Matthew in hinting that we need to catch up on the back story if we are to make sense of Jesus.

Luke, the diligent historian, begins his Gospel by recounting the birth of John the Baptist. Ever the artist, Luke gives us the Old Testament backstory in a more subtle way: through song. When an expectant Mary visits an expectant Elizabeth, she bursts into praise. Her song places her squarely in the context of first-century Jewish anticipation of the Messiah: God "has helped His servant Israel, in remembrance of His mercy, as He spoke to our fathers, to Abraham and to his offspring forever" (1:54–55). Not long after, Zechariah prophesies, reminding us of David and Abraham. So Luke also relates the story of Jesus' birth as the next chapter in a story already in progress.

What about John? The beginning of his Gospel harkens back to the creation narrative of Genesis 1: "In the beginning was the Word." But John also reminds us of Jewish history, telling us that "the law was given through Moses; [but] grace and truth came through Jesus Christ" (John 1:17).

We need to pay attention to these hints we find in the Scriptures. The apostle Paul and each of the Gospel authors (in their own way) point us back to the Old Testament in order to make sense of Jesus. The gospel announcement—as powerful as it is, as central as it is to our faith—needs the gospel story in order to make sense.

Knowing the Backstory

Imagine sitting down for the first time to watch *The Return of the King*, the final film in Tolkien's *The Lord of the Rings* trilogy. You start with the scene that shows Sam and Frodo approaching Mordor. From the music and intensity of the filmmaking, you gather that this must be a key moment in the story. But without any understanding of what has transpired in the past or any knowledge of the shire, the ring, and the importance of these hobbits, you'd be hard pressed to know *why* this moment is so important or how the future of Middle Earth hinges upon Frodo's actions.

Television dramas work the same way. Many of them begin with a brief recap of scenes from previous episodes. The announcer begins by saying, "Previously on . . . " The retrospective clips remind you of the important moments in earlier episodes so that you can better understand what's going on in the current episode.

What do these clips communicate? That you are watching a story. And that if you want to understand what's happening now, you need to know what happened then.

We are two thousand years removed from the story of Jesus. We open up the Gospels and seek to understand them, learn from them, and apply them in a world much different from the one in which they were written. To be able to accomplish this effectively, we must keep the Gospels grounded in history. Without a clear understanding of the historical situation in which this announcement about Jesus is made, we are bound to misunderstand the emphasis of Jesus' message. We may be able to gather a few isolated theological truths, but the focus of the message may be off.

The sweeping story of God and humankind is written on the pages of Scripture, in poems, in psalms, in proverbs, in narrative, and in songs. But all of these genres combine to give us a history, and it is the story we are swept up into by the gracious providence of a loving Creator who desires to be endlessly glorified throughout all eternity.

So the gospel needs the story in order to make sense. The announcement may be glorious and true, but without the surrounding story, it can be misunderstood. It's important that we get the story right; otherwise, we will lose something integral to the plotline and wind up with a counterfeit.

What Is the Gospel Story?

There are four main movements to the gospel story, and these four aspects accomplish several tasks simultaneously.

First, these movements answer key questions: *Where did we come from? What has gone wrong? What is the solution? What is our future?*

Second, each of these movements tells us something about God's character. God reveals Himself through the words He speaks and the actions He takes in each of these scenes.

Third, these movements highlight theological truths that we can state in propositional form. The story brings biblical and systematic theology together, placing propositional truths within a grand narrative. As we watch the story unfold throughout Scripture, we learn about God and ourselves in the process. So let's take a quick journey through the primary scenes of the gospel story.

1. Creation

The opening scenes of the Bible reveal an all-powerful God who speaks and the universe appears out of nothing. At His word, light pierces the darkness. He stretches the sky over the sea. He pulls dry land up out of the ocean and then gently massages it into mountains and valleys, hills and prairies. From the ground spring plants and bushes, solid oak trees and weeping willows, sunflowers and roses.

Like a painter splashing brilliant hues of color onto a canvas, God sends planets spinning and stars whirling into the vast expanse of space. He fills the sky with robins and bluebirds, eagles and seagulls, cardinals and herons. The sea teems with minnows and catfish, dolphins and whales, lobsters and crabs. On the land roam rabbits and horses, ants and elephants, puppies and mountain lions. Over and over again, like an artist admiring his handiwork, God looks at His colorful world and joyfully declares, "It's good!"

Then God made *us*. The first humans, Adam and Eve, lived in perfect harmony with one another and with God. As the pinnacle of God's glorious creation, we were to reflect the image of our Creator. We were given the task of ruling over this world wisely, an act of stewardship for the glory of our king (Genesis 1:28). We were to be mirrors of His majesty and a living testament to the good rule of our Father.

One Hebrew word sums up the picture of Genesis 1 and 2: *shalom*. Peace. Earth was full of God's shalom, the kind of peace in which everything works according to God's intention. The world was made for human flourishing, where we could live in joy in the presence of our Maker, worshiping God by loving Him and one another forever. Looking past all the galaxies and planets, looking through space and time, over and above the exotic creatures that filled the earth, God set His affections on us—His human image-bearers—whom He created to share in the joy of His love forever.

The opening pages of the Bible resonate with us because we know we were made for this kind of world. In *The Weight of Glory*, C. S. Lewis wrote:

> A man's physical hunger does not prove that man will get any bread; he may die of starvation on a raft in the Atlantic. But surely a man's hunger does prove that he comes of a race which repairs its body by eating and inhabits a world where eatable substances exist. In the same way, though I do not believe (I wish I did) that my desire for Paradise proves that I shall enjoy it, I think it a pretty good indication that such a thing exists and that some men will.[2]

The fact that deep down we feel that the world has gone wrong indicates that we were created for a world that is right. The gospel story explains this longing for Eden by telling us that, in the beginning, God created a world that He declared to be good. What does this movement of the story teach us about God?

- He is powerful.
- He is transcendent, directly involved in creation but not part of that creation.
- He is not an impersonal force like that imagined by the creators of *Star Wars,* but a personal being who delights in his creation.
- He is holy—set apart from us, the *Other.* He alone is God.

In the instructions He gives to Adam and Eve, God shows that He is to be glorified through obedience, through our submission to His gracious reign. Therefore, God has authority, the authority to create, to assign tasks, to forbid certain actions. But this kingly authority is not tyrannical or abusive. His authority is forever wed to His love, as a glorious display of fatherly affection for the good world He has created and entrusted to His human image-bearers.

2. Fall

Have you ever noticed how many children's films are about the main character being separated from his or her father? *An American Tail* tells the story of Fievel, a mouse whose curiosity leads him to a forbidden part of a ship full of immigrants. In a terrible storm, Fievel is swept out to sea and spends the rest of the film seeking to be reunited with his papa. When the moment of reunion finally comes, I get teary-eyed even now.

Finding Nemo is about a little fish who rebels against his father's wishes, gets caught by a fisherman, and ends up in an aquarium in a dentist's office. The film shows Nemo's dad, Marlin, traversing the ocean past sharks and jellyfish in order to find his son.

Annie is about an orphan girl longing to be reunited with her parents. *Home Alone* tells the story of a boy who wishes his family were gone (and comes to regret that wish!).

Stories of separation and reunion, exile and return strike a chord in our hearts. Why? Because these stories, in one way or another, mirror the great story of the world, which turns from a shalom-filled world of belonging to a devastating fall that leads to exile.

What happened? Adam and Eve rejected God's rule over them. We refer to their rebellious choice as "the fall," and because they represented all of humanity, their action affects us too. We speak of ourselves as "fallen," having a natural bent toward rebellion from the time we are born. The reason "fall" is an apt description of this event is because it implies that we have descended *from something* or, more accurately put, from *Someone*. We have fallen short of the glory of God.

Even though the world maintains traces of its original beauty, the ugly consequences of our sin have disfigured what was once perfect. Like a broken mirror that distorts the image, we no longer reflect God's glory as we should. Pain and suffering are part of our existence. Death has intruded into the world, and we all are haunted by echoes of the Eden we were forced to abandon.

Sin is a word that is fast disappearing from the modern lexicon. Sometimes even Christians dilute the word's meaning, minimizing the exact nature of what took place in the garden at the dawn of time and what takes place in our lives now as we daily choose our way over God's. We might think of sin as simply making mistakes. Or we might make ourselves out to be victims of suffering and evil. But sin is much more than these things.

Remember the Father who showered the world with His goodness and love in Genesis 1–2? This is the loving Father who owns us, who loves us, who cherishes His creation and seeks its good. He is the Father who watches over us and delights in our finding delight in Him. Yet we have stomped off in defiance and chose to go our own way. We have broken His laws. Every sin we commit is like spraying more graffiti over God's beautiful painting.

Sin is personal. We are guilty of cosmic treason, asserting our own lordship over the lordship of God. We seek worth and value in something other than the Source of all worth. Our hearts are idol-making factories. We seek to worship anything—just not the One who has made us.

Make no mistake. Sin is *ugly*. And until you get a grip on just how ugly our sin is, you will never fully comprehend the gospel story.

The fallout from our sin is devastating. First and foremost, we are guilty before God and alienated from Him. The perfect fellowship that Adam and Eve had with God in the garden of Eden has been broken. We are estranged from our Father. We have—through our attitudes and actions—declared ourselves to be His enemies. This rebellion results in physical and spiritual death.

> AFTER THE FALL, THE EARTH IS SHALOM-SHATTERED.... NATURAL DISASTERS SWEEP OVER OUR LANDS. NATIONS RISE AGAINST NATION. DEATH SNATCHES OUR LOVED ONES.

Our broken relationship with God sends repercussions into all of society. We war against each other. We fight for recognition. The pride that would have us dethrone God is the same pride that keeps others at arm's length. We are suspicious and angry, bitter and envious, deceived and deceiving.

We are plagued by shame and guilt—ashamed because our ability to reflect God has now been distorted, guilty because we have raged against our Creator in a remarkable display of rebellion. The evil of our sin attracts His personal, white-hot wrath. Ironically, our innate sense of justice causes us to long for God to be wrathful, to judge this evil. But we often fail to realize that for

God's justice to be enforced, we too must come under His judgment. All of us are guilty.

At the time of creation, the earth is shalom-filled. After the fall, the earth is shalom-shattered. God's intent to have humans rule the world rightly has been, temporarily, put on hold. Now, work is toilsome. Childbirth is painful. Natural disasters sweep over our lands. Nations rise against nation. Death snatches away our loved ones, and we sense its unrelenting approach hot upon our own necks as well. Even the created order groans under the weight of our sin.

The fall shows us that God takes sin seriously. He hates sin for what it does to us and to His good creation. He also hates sin because it is personally directed against Him and denies the honor that is due Him. He is firmly committed to upholding the glory of His name, for when His name is glorified, His people find their fullest joy in Him.

3. Redemption

Thankfully, the loving Creator who rightly shows Himself to be wrathful toward our sin is determined to turn the evil and suffering we have caused into good that will be to His ultimate glory. So the next movement in the gospel story shows God implementing a master plan for redeeming His world and rescuing fallen sinners. He will restore everything that our sin has broken.

Gospel storytellers too often jump from the garden of Eden to the death of Jesus on the cross. But the narrative of redemption doesn't begin in the New Testament. God reveals His rescue plan just after He exiles Adam and Eve from the garden. He promises that one of Eve's descendants will make right what she and Adam have done wrong.

The launch of God's plan takes place most clearly in Genesis 12. God chooses the patriarch, Abraham, to become the father of a great nation. Through Abraham's family (particularly, one of Abraham's descendants), God promises to bring blessing to all the nations of the world. Though Abraham and his wife are elderly and past the years of childbearing, they take God at His word, believing that God can bring life from a dead womb. That kind of resurrection faith forms the heart of the people of God.

The rest of the Old Testament tells the story of God's chosen people, Israel. God acts on their behalf, rescuing them from slavery and bringing them to the Promised Land. God gives them the law to govern their lives together and to reveal the character of the holy God they serve.

All the seemingly needless details of the Old Testament actually serve the plotline of the Scriptures. In the temple worship, the office of the priesthood, the sacrificial systems, and the covenant that God makes with His people, we learn more and more about the rescue that God is planning.

But Israel, though called to be the people of God on behalf of this fallen world, cannot provide redemption. God's people are part of the problem. The law, though given by God for the good of His people, exposes human sinfulness and every person's need for God's righteousness. The sacrifices, though commanded by God, can never pay the price for human sin. They serve only to point forward to the perfect Lamb who will come to take away the sins of the world. Though appointed by God to rule wisely over His people, the kings of Judah and Israel demonstrate that they are far from being the King who will bring blessing to all nations through wholehearted devotion to God.

In the history of Israel, we see a pattern develop: blessing, rebellion, exile, return. God blesses; the people rebel; they are exiled; God brings them back. At the end of the Old Testament, Israel is nearly destroyed. The faithful remnant is exiled. And even as the people of God slowly find their way back to the Promised Land, they remain under foreign rule. They are longing once again for God to act, for God to bring about the climax of His long-promised plan to restore the world.

The Old Testament is a story in search of an ending. The final pages show the people of God as scattered, waiting for redemption, hoping that God will act again to save them. The world continues to cry and groan under the weight of God's divine curse. The plan of redemption cannot go forward. God's reign—His kingdom—cannot be reestablished in the way He first intended unless a faithful, sinless human being was to offer the obedience required, pay the necessary penalty for sin (death), and be exalted as king over creation.

GOD COMES TO HIS PEOPLE [NOT] AS THE GREAT JUDGE [BUT] AS THE SUFFERING SERVANT.

Enter Jesus. At just the right time and in just the right place, God comes to His people. But He doesn't come as the great Judge, purging the Promised Land of foreigners and reestablishing David's throne in Jerusalem. He first comes as the suffering servant.

In the Person of Jesus Christ, God Himself comes to renew the world and restore His people. The grand narrative of Scripture climaxes with the death and resurrection of Jesus. By submitting Himself to His Father's will, even to the point of dying on the cross, Jesus undoes the curse of Adam. This Messiah-King takes upon Himself the punishment for human sin. His atoning sacrifice reconciles us to God, inaugurates His kingdom, and becomes the means by which we are remade into God's image. Jesus fulfills—through His perfect life of obedience, death in the place of sinners, and resurrection to new life—all that is necessary for God's rescue plan to be put into motion.

We will unpack the specifics of this gospel announcement in more detail in part 2. Right now, it is important to note that the way we can be caught up into this great story of redemption is by repenting of sin and trusting in Jesus.

4. Restoration

The story doesn't end with redemption. God has promised to renew the whole world, and the Bible gives us a peek into this glorious future.

I remember with fond memories going to visit my grandparents as a child. My grandmother is an excellent cook, and we would visit once a week to have a meal together. From the moment we drove up to the house, we were greeted by the smells of the feast wafting into the driveway. The roast beef was cooking, and the cornbread was in the oven. Once I got a whiff of that fragrance, my stomach would begin growling. I knew what was coming!

In a far greater way, Christians are to live in the present by anticipating what God has promised in the future. We can smell the fragrance of new creation. The restoration of the world has already begun, but has not yet fully taken place. Through the death and resurrection of Jesus, the life of heaven has invaded earth. The kingdom of God has begun to advance.

GOD PROMISES THE DAY IS COMING WHEN THERE WILL BE NO MORE . . . HIDDEN TEARS AND UNANSWERED QUESTIONS.

God has given us the Holy Spirit as the down payment on the future (see Ephesians 1:13–14). The Holy Spirit is the guarantee of what will eventually be a reality for all who believe in Jesus: a new heaven and new earth in which righteousness dwells (2 Peter 3:13).

God promises that the day is coming when there will be no more sickness and pain, no more sorrow and suffering, no more hidden tears and unanswered questions. The Russian novelist, Fyodor Dostoevsky pictured restoration this way:

> I have a childlike conviction that the sufferings will be healed and smoothed over, that the whole offensive comedy of human contradictions will disappear like a pitiful mirage . . . and

that ultimately, at the world's finale, in the moment of eternal harmony, there will occur and be revealed something so precious that it will suffice for all hearts, to allay all indignation, to redeem all human villainy, all bloodshed; it will suffice not only to make forgiveness possible, but also to justify everything that has happened with men.[3]

God is working in human history to make all things new. And nowhere is this more evident than in His initiative to call out a people—the church—and make them new by the power of His Spirit. The church is made up of those who have repented of their sins and trusted in the good news of Jesus Christ, specifically that Christ has died for our sins and been raised from the dead. When we place our faith in the crucified and risen king, we receive eternal life, the life of the promised world to come.

As the citizens of the kingdom that is coming, we become the presence of the future world. We don't build the kingdom or bring the kingdom, but we do seek to faithfully witness to the kingdom. And through His people, God continues to implement the victory Christ achieved on the cross. So we long with eager expectation for the day when the kingdoms of this world will become the kingdom of our Lord and of His Christ.

The restoration of all things will take place in two ways. Christ will return to judge sin and evil, and He will usher in righteousness and peace. God will purge this world of evil once and for all. Since all of us long for justice, this truth causes our hearts to leap for joy. But since all of us are also sinners, this truth strikes terror as well. How will we survive?

The only way to escape the fair and furious judgment of God is to be on the side of justice on that day of reckoning, and the only way to be on the side of justice is by acknowledging our sentence served by Jesus' death and accepting our vindication proclaimed through His resurrection.

Key Answers to Deep Questions

Herman Bavinck, a Dutch theologian, once summed up the gospel story this way: "God the Father has reconciled His created but fallen world through the death of His Son, and renews it into a Kingdom of God by His Spirit."[4]

The gospel story answers the deep philosophical and spiritual questions that people wonder about: *How did we get here? Are people basically good or evil? Is there hope in this world? What happens when someone dies? What does the future hold?*

Apart from Christ, these questions cannot be answered consistently. That is why we as Christians must be bold enough to provide answers to these questions and expect the Holy Spirit to confirm these truths in the hearts of unbelievers.

This gospel story provides purpose for us here today. Over and over again in the Bible, we see how God uses actions and events intended for evil to bring about good. At the center of this narrative, we have the cross of Christ, where—within the greatest evil ever committed—God the Son provides the sacrifice for human sin and becomes the catalyst for cosmic restoration.

The gospel story also answers the longing that we have to be part of a story bigger than our personal stories but which is able to incorporate and add meaning to our individual experiences. Life is not random and meaningless. God tells us (and shows us) that there is a divine purpose at work behind all that takes place.

This desire for meaning and purpose behind our individual stories is wired into us as humans. The stories of this world can never succeed at tying all our individual stories together into one great meta-narrative. But where the world's great stories fail, the gospel story succeeds.

We are part of a story that is about Jesus Christ, the King of the universe. The slain Lamb is the conquering King—through whom and for whom our world exists.

Ironically, when we live as if our personal story is at the center of our universe, we struggle to find meaning and significance. But when Christ is at the center and we are pushed to the periphery, it is then—in that place of seeming obscurity and insignificance— that we find true worth and value, by giving glory to the crucified and risen King with whom we can become united through faith.

At the great finale of the history of this world, when the King returns and subdues everything under his feet, all of our unanswered questions will be resolved in light of the God who comes to dwell with man and wipe every tear from every eye.

C. S. Lewis called this new world "Chapter One of the Great Story which no one on earth has read: which goes on forever; in which every chapter is better than the one before."[5]

Scripture Truths

THE GOSPEL ANNOUNCEMENT IN THE CONTEXT OF THE GOSPEL STORY: *Matthew 1:1-17; Mark 1:1-3; Luke 1; John 1:1-18; 1 Corinthians 15:1-4; Hebrews 11*

CREATION: *Genesis 1–2; Psalm 19:1–4*

FALL: *Genesis 3; Romans 1:18–32; 3:9–20*

REDEMPTION: *Genesis 12; 17:1–10; Exodus 12; 2 Samuel 7; Isaiah 42:1–4; 53:4–11; Matthew 26–28; Mark 14–16; Luke 22–24; John 1:1–18; 3:1–21; Acts 2; Romans 3; Ephesians 2:1–10*

RESTORATION: *Acts 1:6–11; Romans 8; Ephesians 1; 1 Thessalonians 4:13–5:11; Hebrews 12:18–29; 2 Peter 3:1–13; Revelation 21–22*

To know the glories of Christ is an end, not a means.

– John Piper

the therapeutic gospel

A FEW YEARS ago, I watched a television documentary about the work of several doctors in an emergency room. A woman came in, coughing uncontrollably. As one of the doctors talked to her, he found out that she had been a smoker for many years. He prescribed some medicine that would temporarily relieve the worst of her coughing, but he told her that the cough would not completely go away as long as she continued smoking. A few weeks later, the lady came back, complaining that the medicine was no longer working. The doctor again explained, "I'm only addressing your symptom. The real problem is that you continue to damage your lungs."

Every doctor knows that getting the diagnosis right is vitally important for giving the right prescription. It isn't enough to treat symptoms; doctors must identify the root cause of a patient's problem.

As Christians, we should be no less vigilant in searching the

Scriptures for the true diagnosis of our spiritual state. In busy emergency rooms, some doctors may feel pressured to hand out medicine in order to clear the board and lighten the patient load. Busy pastors and teachers may feel a similar pressure—to proclaim a gospel that temporarily relieves painful symptoms, but fails to address root causes. When doctors treat symptoms without ever looking for a cause, they are accused of medical malpractice. But when pastors deliver a message that only treats symptoms and makes people feel better temporarily, they are applauded and lifted up as an example for everyone else.

The Therapeutic Gospel

The first counterfeit we will look at distorts the gospel story we looked at in the last chapter. Remember the main movements of the story? *Creation, fall, redemption, restoration.* This counterfeit targets "the fall." But, as we'll see, once you change the Bible's view of the fall, you wind up with an altered understanding of redemption too.

We call this counterfeit "the therapeutic gospel" because it confuses our spiritual symptoms (a troubled marriage, anxiety, anger, addictions) with our spiritual disease (sin). Because the diagnosis is superficial, the treatment is also superficial.

The therapeutic gospel answers a key question like, *What are we here for?* by pointing to our desire for personal happiness. Another important question, *What has gone wrong?* is answered by pointing to our feelings of emptiness. Sin is recast as an obstacle to finding happiness. It's whatever gets in the way of our becoming all that we ought to be. God wants to patch up the hole in our hearts, and He does this by sending Jesus to fill our hearts with love and to bless our pursuit of happiness. The church is then transformed into a place to help people find personal fulfillment.

Evangelical Versions of the Therapeutic Gospel

Though we as evangelicals claim to take the Word of God seriously, we are not immune to this counterfeit gospel. Here are some ways that the therapeutic gospel seeps into our churches:

The Happy Meal Gospel

From the time our son was a toddler, he knew McDonald's and why he wanted to go there. The playground was a draw, for sure, but the Happy Meal sealed the deal. No other fast food option compared to Chicken Nuggets and a toy. Promise a child a toy and you capture his heart!

The brilliance of the Happy Meal comes from its promise not only of the toy, but of happiness. The mere thought of a McDonald's Happy Meal lights up a child's face. Parents aren't just purchasing greasy chicken and soggy French fries; they are purchasing an *experience* that will make their kids feel good.

Sometimes we package the gospel in a way that makes God out to be a kind of Ronald McDonald who wants to give kids a Happy Meal. We make "pursuing happiness" the central goal of life, and we work toward this goal by being nice and helpful to other people. Whenever we do have conflicts, we resolve them quickly so we can restore our own peace of mind. As peace of mind becomes the goal of the Christian life, the idea that we would need peace with God slowly becomes incomprehensible. (After all, what could Ronald McDonald possibly have against me?)

How do you know whether you've fallen for the Happy Meal gospel? One very practical way is to examine your prayer life. When are you most likely to go to God in prayer? What kinds of requests do you make? Is your biggest concern your unmet emotional needs? Or are you concerned about how your life reflects the glory of God?

It's easy to criticize the obvious displays of the Happy Meal god. But too often we fail to see our own pursuit of God as an avenue to self-fulfillment. We unintentionally look to God as a tool for bringing the happiness we think will be ours when we are at the center of the universe.

A few years ago, a Nicholas Sparks book entitled *A Walk to Remember* was made into a movie. The film tells the story of a Christian girl who befriends a young man in need of grace. The movie appealed to evangelicals because it showed Christians in a positive light by lifting up the young girl as a role model whose faith influenced her life.

Unfortunately, the therapeutic gospel tainted this film. In one particular scene, the young girl is on the front porch of her home, debating with her father (a pastor) about the wisdom of dating an unbeliever. Her father says, "You might not care what I say or think. But you should care about God's opinion." She replies, "I think God wants me to be happy."

End of discussion. "God wants me to be happy" trumps all the debate over whether it is biblically right or wrong for a Christian to date an unbeliever.

When "God wants me to be happy" becomes the measuring stick for making decisions, we have fallen for a counterfeit. The tragedy of the therapeutic gospel is that it affirms the wrong concepts with the right words. God *does* want us to be happy, but not in a way defined by twenty-first-century American culture. God's desire for our joy goes beyond the Happy Meal.

The Fill 'er Up Gospel

Another variation of the therapeutic gospel imagines that our problem is like a car running low on gasoline. We are empty and need to be filled. Our self-image is poor, and we lack self-esteem. We wallow needlessly in feelings of guilt and unworthiness. God is there to fill up our depleted reservoir until we are restored to full emotional health. The church is like a gas station where we are recharged and refueled.

In this version of the therapeutic gospel, the concept of sin refers to anything that would make people doubt their inherent worth and beauty. Sin is our lack of self-esteem. So pastors are there to encourage us with statements like:

"There is a hero within you awaiting to be awakened."

"The real problem is that deep down we feel we're not good enough to approach a holy God."

"Sin is any act or thought that robs myself or another human being of his or her self-esteem."

Notice what has taken place here. Instead of understanding that our sin *may lead* to a lack of self-esteem, sin has *become* low self-esteem. Instead of understanding that our sin *leads to* feelings of guilt and shame, sin has *become* those feelings. It's a classic case of confusing the symptom with the cause.

The therapeutic solution is to minimize the biblical understanding of sin (rebellion against God) by saying, "Let's focus on the positive! Sin and judgment shouldn't be our message. People already feel bad. Why beat them down with words like 'sin'?"

Such talk sounds very merciful. But notice what solution is offered: *Do better. Feel better about yourself. Try harder. Believe you can succeed.* The underlying message is clear: *God will fill you up, but it's your job to change!*

The Fill 'er Up gospel sounds positive on the surface, but beneath the glitz and the glamour is a negative, unmerciful message. Like telling a clinically depressed person, "Just snap out of it!" the therapeutic gospel offers people burdened by sin and guilt *more* reason to despair. It's like giving sugar to a diabetic, telling people that the magic medicine will help them, when it is, in fact, speeding up their demise.

In her autobiography, Lucille Ball, early television's most successful comedienne, admits that during the peak of *I Love Lucy*, she felt guilt-ridden and anxious. A friend introduced her to a

New York pastor known for promoting positive thinking. Ball went to this pastor for counseling about her feelings of guilt. What a grand opportunity to take someone to the cross, to provide the message of forgiveness and grace that changes the heart and soothes the mind! But according to Ball, the pastor gave no such message. His advice? Just stop feeling guilty! "Is it right for you to worry about your children? You wouldn't have them if God didn't want you to and if he didn't feel you deserved them."[1]

This version of the therapeutic gospel misdiagnoses our problem at a fundamental level. Scripture is clear that our biggest problem is not that we *feel* guilty; it's that we *are* guilty. It's not that we have a low view of ourselves; it's that we have too low a view of *God*. Our hearts are not empty. They are already filled with all sorts of cancerous sinful desires that needed to be rooted out. We don't have depleted hearts in need of a fill-up; we have deceitful hearts in need of replacement.

In the end, if low self-esteem is the problem, then therapy is the solution. The questions for Christians then become: Why do we need Jesus? Why is a bloody cross at the center of our faith? If our biggest need is to feel good about ourselves, God could have sent Oprah. If our big need is to get along with our family, God could have sent Dr. Phil. But if God sent his Son to die a brutal, horrifying death as a payment for human sin, then surely our sin must be much more heinous than "feeling empty inside."

The Fill 'er Up gospel twists the meaning of Jesus' death into something unrecognizable. It makes Christ's death all about magnifying *our* worth before God, proving to us how valuable and precious we are, when the biblical understanding of Christ's death should instead magnify God and His mercy.

The Paid Programming Gospel

Paid programming on television usually comes in a thirty-minute format and offers a consumerist vision of salvation. You diagnose a problem, and you introduce your product as the solution to the problem. Then you put on display all the ways that the item adds benefit and value to your life.

When I was a teenager, one of my chores was to mop the kitchen floor every day. We had a little television set on the counter in the kitchen, so I could watch TV while I cleaned up. One day, an infomercial came on. The salespeople were promoting a revolutionary new mop that would last for ages and even keep the bucket water clean. I was mesmerized. That afternoon, I begged my mom to let me throw away our old mop and get the one I'd seen on TV. She let me call the 800 number, and I ordered that mop right away. After it  came, I used it once or twice before realizing that it was just another mop. It wasn't any worse than my old one, but it wasn't any better either. Early on, I learned a valuable lesson that I can't believe everything I see on television.

THE THERAPEUTIC GOSPEL CAN'T DELIVER THE CHANGE . . . BECAUSE IT DOESN'T RECOGNIZE THE SEVERITY OF THE PROBLEM.

Sadly, you can't always believe everything you hear in church either. Sometimes our church services resemble an hour-long version of paid programming in which we communicate a message that says, *Come to Jesus, and your life will get better!* The problem is that your life stinks. The good news is that Jesus can turn it around!

Of course, there is truth in saying that life gets better when one trusts in Jesus. But what is "better"? Without defining what "better" looks like, we leave the door open for Jesus to become just an accessory, an addition to an old way of life. The church begins to sound like an infomercial. Name your problem, and Jesus is the answer.

Despite the rhetoric, simply adding Jesus to your life *as it is* will not bring total transformation. The therapeutic gospel can't deliver the change it promises, mainly because it doesn't recognize the severity of the problem.

Imagine this scenario. You live in a house near a river. A terrible storm comes, and the river floods your neighborhood and your home. Days later, volunteers descend upon the area, seeking to help anyone in need. If you've ever been involved in disaster relief, you know what must be done. You've got to shovel the mud out of your home. You've got to tear out the dry wall (all the way to the ceiling, since the moisture seeps up through the walls). All the furniture must be replaced. The air conditioning ducts under the house must be thrown away. Wood floors must be pulled up and replaced. Just about everything in the house must be replaced.

The volunteers tell you, "Don't worry! Things look bad in here, but we can help. We'll have this place fixed in no time!" You are grateful for the good news. But as the day goes on, you notice that the volunteers are acting oddly. They aren't spending much time in the house. Instead, they are building a screened-in porch that connects to the house. At the end of the day, they smile and say, "We told you things would be better!"

You look at the house and can still smell the mold. Nothing has been done to deal with the major problems. Sure, the addition of a screened-in porch is a nice touch, but *that's not what you need.*

The therapeutic gospel, particularly the paid programming version, says that when you come to Jesus, your life will get better. But rather than seeing Jesus as a master builder who can rip up the moldy, rotting wood and make it all new, the therapeutic gospel envisions Him as more of a pleasant volunteer who simply builds an addition to an existing structure.

The "good news" of the therapeutic gospel is that you're not as bad as you think you are. Neither is the solution as radical as you might have expected. Come to Jesus, and He will make some home improvements!

God as the Vending Machine

The most extreme form of the therapeutic gospel is what is often called "the prosperity gospel." Put simply, it teaches that God is obligated to bless you for your obedience. God is the great bargainer. You do your part, and God will do His.

God is like a vending machine. You put in your token, and then you get your candy bar. Thankfully, many evangelicals see right through this counterfeit. But more subtle versions of this teaching permeate our churches.

Take tithing, for example. Some churches challenge their people to tithe for ninety days, agreeing to offer church members their money back if they haven't felt God's blessing during that time. Many tithing stories go something like this: "We decided to tithe, and now look how much money God has given us!" It may be a more subtle form of the prosperity gospel, but it's still as if God is a vending machine. Instead of giving from a generous heart, overwhelmed by gratitude for God's grace, our "generosity" becomes a way to *get* something from God.

Likewise, some of us may go on short-term mission trips as a way of bargaining with God. We sacrifice for a few days in order to receive a mountaintop spiritual experience from God. While I would never deny the blessing that comes from missions (I've tasted that blessing many times!), our mission activities ought to always be motivated by thankful hearts for the great reward of salvation we have already received through Christ's obedience.

Or perhaps we volunteer and help in church activities, hoping that God will bless our faithfulness and give us what we want in other areas of life. We must be careful that our service is always rooted in love for our brothers and sisters, or else we will short-circuit the great blessings God wants to give us.

The problem with the Vending Machine gospel, in whatever form it takes, is that God can *never* be put in our debt. God never owes us anything. It inverts our relationship to God, making him out to be a puppet whose strings are pulled by our actions.

the therapeutic gospel

STORY	ANNOUNCEMENT	COMMUNITY
The fall is seen as the failure of humans to reach our potential. Sin is primarily about us, as it robs us of our sense of fullness.	Christ's death proves our inherent worth as human beings and gives us the power to reach our full potential.	The church helps us along in our quest for personal happiness and vocational fulfillment.

Why This Counterfeit is Attractive

It's always good to ask why a counterfeit is attractive. The only way that a counterfeit can fool people is that it looks much like the real thing. You won't find counterfeit $100 bills that picture Benjamin Franklin with a mustache. That would be too obvious. Counterfeit bills are always subtle. The same is true for counterfeit gospels. There must be something here that resembles the true gospel; otherwise, people would never fall for it. Here are some things the therapeutic gospel gets right:

The therapeutic gospel rightly insists upon human worth.
Just like the gospel story says, human beings are the pinnacle of God's creation. We are made in His image. Humans have an intrinsic worth and value due to our special status bestowed on us by God. Human life is sacred, and we have been given special responsibilities before God.

The therapeutic gospel affirms what we all know to be true: *Humans are valuable.* We have innate worth that is given to us by God. That worth is not the cause of our salvation, as we will soon see. But this counterfeit rightly understands that God is interested in us and our lives.

The therapeutic gospel says that God comforts us in our time of need.

Numerous psalms refer to God as our comfort and help in time of trouble. How marvelous that we can lean hard on the everlasting arms of God during the turbulent times in our life! God *is* there for us in our time of need. There are times when we don't sense His presence as much as we'd like to, but the fact remains: God is there.

The therapeutic gospel rightly understands that God showers us with His affection and love, especially in those times when we need to sense His fatherly care.

The therapeutic gospel tells us that God keeps His promises.

In the Old Testament, God blessed the patriarchs with long life and wealth. The psalmist points to success and prosperity as signs of God's blessing. God makes promises to His people, and as a faithful God, He always delivers those promises.

In the New Testament, the church also receives promises from God. God promises to wipe away every tear from our eyes. He has promised us eternal life. We look forward to a day when pain will be no more, and suffering and heavenly riches will be ours in Christ.

The therapeutic gospel is right to focus our attention on these promises. The problem is not that this counterfeit leads us to hopes that are too high; it's that these hopes are not high enough. They leave us in a state of longing for provision, rather than longing for the God from whom all blessings flow.

The Results of the Therapeutic Gospel

Whenever the therapeutic gospel takes hold, certain results are bound to follow. These results leave us spiritually anemic at just the time we need to be spiritually empowered. Here are three main results that come from the therapeutic gospel:

Disillusionment When Suffering Comes

If you believe that coming to Christ will make life easier and better, then you will be disappointed when suffering comes your way. Storms destroy our homes. Cancer eats up our bodies. Economic recessions steal our jobs.

If you see God as a vending machine, then you will become disillusioned when your candy bar doesn't drop. You may get angry and want to start banging on the machine. Or maybe you will be plagued with guilt, convinced that your suffering indicates God's disapproval of something you've done.

GOD IS NOT INTERESTED IN OUR SELF-ACTUALIZATION; HE'S INTERESTED IN OUR SPIRIT-ACTUALIZATION.

When we emphasize the temporal blessings that come from following Christ, we plant the seeds for a harvest of heartbreak. Christians who languish in poverty wonder if perhaps they are simply not as faithful as those who have riches. Believers who are slowly losing their battle with sickness wonder why their faith hasn't healed them. Those who linger around the edges of depression wonder why the happy, peppy Christian life they were promised continues to elude them.

Disillusionment always comes in the wake of the therapeutic gospel. Why? Because the New Testament focuses on the glory of Christ, not the glory of health and wealth. Trusting Christ leads us to deny ourselves and follow a crucified Man of Sorrows, One acquainted with grief. It seems counterintuitive, but it's in *renouncing* our right to happiness that we receive the greatest joy from God.

We long for happiness, yes. But true happiness does not line up with the world's definition. True joy is much deeper and richer than that offered by the various versions of the therapeutic gospel, because true joy is found in God Himself, not just in His gifts.

The god of the therapeutic gospel is too small. We think that because God is love, we will be delivered from trials and discomfort. But God loves us too much to only give us comfort and prosperity.

God is not interested in our self-actualization; He's interested in our Spirit-actualization. He is forming us into the image of His Son. And if we are to look more like Jesus, the Suffering Servant, surely we will pass through times of suffering.

A Shrunken View of Sin

The therapeutic gospel neglects the idea of sin as rebellion against God. Instead, sin is seen as acting against one's own good. Sin is ultimately directed at you yourself.

On the surface, it's attractive to think that we're really not as bad as we think we are. The therapeutic gospel offers a much more optimistic view of human nature, suggesting that we are mostly good.

But this understanding of sin actually robs us of the beauty of God's grace. What looks more glorious? A God who loves us by ignoring our sin? Or a God who pays the enormous debt for our sin by taking it upon Himself? When sin is seen as the rebellion it is, grace is costly—and transformative! When sin is shrunken to the point that our accountability to God is removed, then grace is cheap, and it leaves us unchanged.

Ironically, it's the therapeutic understanding of sin that leaves us with low self-esteem. We begin to compare ourselves to others. We interpret our circumstances as evidence of how well we must be doing in God's eyes. The therapeutic gospel exacerbates our desire to measure up, which then leads to greater guilt.

Make sin an external problem, and you give people an internal heartache. But once you realize that sin is an internal problem, you can point people to an external solution. We need God to swoop down and save us. The biblical gospel tells us that our greatest problem is *us* and that our great salvation is God.

We are rebellious sinners, but God loves us anyway. God's love for me is greater and more impressive because of how bad I am, not because I'm okay.

People Who Desire What God Can Give Us Rather Than God Himself

The therapeutic gospel ultimately fails to satisfy because it switches out the great reward of knowing God with the lesser reward of receiving something from God. God's good gifts are intended to lead us to Him. Our goal is not to receive a reward from God; it's to receive *God himself!*

The saddest result of the therapeutic gospel is that it produces disciples who are more interested in the gifts than the Giver. Even a gift like heaven can be twisted into something that competes with God for our affections. If our primary reason to get saved is to go to heaven and avoid hell, we have trusted in Christ *for something He can give us* rather than for who He is Himself.

Of course, there are many rewards for following Christ. Peace in the midst of the storm is one of them. It's also true that God blesses those who give generously, since our generosity can become a funnel through which God distributes *His* money to other people through us. God blesses those who serve His church, who join His mission, and who follow Him in obedience.

But we don't obey in order to receive earthly rewards. This inverts the gospel. We obey out of love for our great king in the present, out of gratitude for the salvation He has granted us in the past, and out of faith in the mercy of God for the future.

Christ has not come to help you find satisfaction in a pain-free life here and now. He has come to give you satisfaction *in Him.* The therapeutic gospel makes salvation about you and your happiness apart from God's glory. The biblical gospel makes salvation about God's glory, and it is in seeking that glory that we find true and lasting happiness.

Charles Spurgeon once told a memorable story that illustrates the difference between loving and selfish motives:

There once was a gardener who grew an enormous carrot. So he took it to his King and said, "My Lord, this is the greatest carrot I've ever grown or ever will grow. Therefore, I want to present it to you as a token of my love and respect for you." The King was touched and discerned the man's heart. So as he turned to go, the King said, "Wait! You are clearly a good steward of the earth. I own a plot of land right next to yours. I want to give it to you freely as a gift so you can garden it all." And the gardener was amazed and delighted and went home rejoicing.

But there was a nobleman at the King's court who overheard all this, and he said, "My! If that is what you get for a *carrot*— what if you gave the King something better?" So the next day the nobleman came before the king, and he was leading a handsome black stallion. He bowed low and said, "My Lord, I breed horses and this is the greatest horse I've ever bred or ever will breed. Therefore I want to present it to you as a token of my love and respect for you." But the King discerned his heart and said, "Thank you." And he took the horse and merely dismissed him.

The nobleman was perplexed. So the King said, "Let me explain. That Gardener was giving *me* a carrot. But you were giving your*self* a horse."[2]

Countering the Counterfeit

So what do we do if we have fallen for the therapeutic gospel? How do we counter the effects of the therapeutic gospel when we run into them? Here are three suggestions:

Put God in the Center

In the mid-1990s, Jim Carrey starred in a movie called *The Truman Show*. The film parodied the rise of reality television shows, casting Carrey as the prime actor in a 24/7 reality show broadcast around the world. Everything in Truman's world revolves around Truman, but eventually he catches on and realizes something is wrong.

This film has led to an interesting psychosis that doctors are calling "The Truman Show Delusion," in which patients believe they are the prime actors in a 24/7 reality television show. One patient said this: "I realized that I was and am the center, the focus of attention for millions and millions of people. . . . My family and everyone I knew were and are actors in a script, a charade whose entire purpose is to make me the focus of the world's attention."[3] Wow! Talk about thinking you're the center of the universe!

We laugh at this kind of self-centeredness, but then we turn right around and adopt the therapeutic gospel, which puts us in the center of the world. Many of us imagine the world as if we were at the center, but unlike Truman, we never realize that something is amiss.

According to the Bible, we find meaning, purpose, and fulfillment in *not* being at the center of the universe. It is when we discover God at the center of our universe that we find our proper place. The therapeutic gospel is inherently human-centered. The biblical gospel is God-centered. It's not primarily about your happiness or fulfillment. It's about God and His glory. Once you see God for who He is, you are delivered from self-centeredness and are free to drink from the deep wells of joy and contentment that come from knowing Him.

Find Your Joy in God Alone

Another way to counter the therapeutic gospel is to find satisfaction in God Himself, even as you walk through times of terrible suffering. The therapeutic gospel makes Christ a tool for getting something else. The biblical gospel says, "Christ is all."

The writer of Hebrews commends his readers, saying, "You joyfully accepted the plundering of your property, since you knew that you yourselves had a better possession and an abiding one" (Hebrews 10:34). The therapeutic gospel has no category for pleasing God through times of suffering, because pain is always somehow caused by our own lack of faith. And yet the writer to the Hebrews can commend people for joyfully losing everything because their ultimate treasure was God alone.

What kind of gospel would lead someone to be joyful, even in the midst of great earthly loss? Not the therapeutic gospel. Only the biblical gospel that magnifies Jesus Christ as the treasure of greatest worth can lead someone to great joy in the midst of great loss.

The most prolific Romanian hymn writer of the twentieth century was Nicolae Moldoveanu. He wrote thousands of hymns during his long life, composing many of them in prison as he suffered at the hands of the communist authorities. One of Moldoveanu's most beloved songs, "Tie-Ti Cant Dumnezeul Meu" ("To You I Sing My God," 1983), was written just after the police had plundered his home and left him without any belongings. Only someone gripped by the biblical gospel could pen such words of trust, including, "For all that you have given to me, / for your sweet care, / For all that you have taken from me, / I worship you with thanksgiving."

Find Your Worth in the Gospel

The therapeutic gospel leads us to believe that our own worth is the motivation for God's saving action. According to this line of thinking, Christ came to save us because we were so valuable to God. This teaching sounds very attractive, but it more closely resembles ancient Gnosticism than biblical Christianity. A good example comes from comparing the parable of the lost sheep in the Gospel of Luke and the gnostic Gospel of Thomas (written long after our canonical Gospels). Luke's version of Jesus' parable of the lost sheep goes like this:

> What man of you, having a hundred sheep, if he has lost one of them, does not leave the ninety-nine in the open country, and go after the one that is lost, until he finds it? And when he has found it, he lays it on his shoulders, rejoicing. And when he comes home, he calls together his friends and his neighbors, saying to them, "Rejoice with me, for I have found my sheep that was lost!" Just so, I tell you, there will be more joy in heaven over one sinner who repents than over ninety-nine righteous persons who need no repentance. (Luke 15:4–7)

Notice the version found in the non-biblical Gospel of Thomas:

> Jesus said, "The Kingdom is like a shepherd who had a hundred sheep. One of them, the largest went astray. He left the ninety-nine and sought the one until he found it. After he had gone to this trouble, he said to the sheep, "I love you more than the ninety-nine."[4]

What's the difference between Luke's version of this parable and the version that appears in the Gospel of Thomas? In the non-biblical version, the author has made the parable about the *worth* of the sheep instead of the *work* of the shepherd. The second version imagines that the sheep was sought because it was so valuable.

But Scripture tells us something different. The point of salvation is not that God loves us because we are valuable. The point of salvation is that *God* is the greatest, and in His mercy He has chosen to give us worth by loving us when we had nothing in us deserving salvation.

The therapeutic gospel leaves us thinking, "Lord, thanks for recognizing my worth and loving me!" The biblical gospel leaves us on our knees in profound gratitude, crying, "Thank You, God, that even though my heart is more like a defaced rock than a precious jewel, You saw fit to love me."

The therapeutic gospel says, "I am valuable, and that's why God loves me." The biblical gospel says, "I am valuable *because* God loves me!"

Once you grasp the truth that there is nothing intrinsically worthy in yourself that would cause God to act on your behalf, you are overwhelmed by grace flowing from a God who chose to reach down and deliver you anyway. And all you can repeat through tears is, "Why me? Why me? Why me? Such amazing grace! Why would He save a wretch like me?"

The therapeutic gospel makes grace expected. The biblical gospel makes grace amazing.

Scripture Truths

ON THE COSTS OF DISCIPLESHIP: *Matthew 7:14; Luke 9:62; 14:26–28, 31, 33*

ON HUMAN WORTH: *Genesis 1:26–31; 9:6; Psalm 8:4–5; Proverbs 24:11–12; Jeremiah 1:4–5; Matthew 6:26*

ON GOD AS OUR HELP IN TIMES OF TROUBLE: *Exodus 15; Psalm 23; 46; Isaiah 40:1–8; 61; Philippians 4:4–7*

ON SUFFERING AS A WAY OF BEING CONFORMED INTO THE IMAGE OF CHRIST: *2 Corinthians 11; Colossians 1:24–2:5; Hebrews 12:1–17; James 1:2–4; 1 Peter 1:3–9; 4:12–19; Hebrews 10:34*

ON THE PERVASIVENESS OF SIN: *Psalm 14:1–3; 53:1–3; Isaiah 64:6; Jeremiah 17:9; Matthew 15:19*

ON THE LOVE OF GOD FOR SINNERS: *Mark 2:13–17; 8:1–3; Luke 15; John 13:1; Romans 5:6–11; 1 Timothy 1:12–17*

Love in action is a harsh and dreadful thing,
compared with love in dreams.

– **Fyodor Dostoevsky,** *The Brothers Karamazov*

the judgmentless gospel

JOHN LENNON'S 1971 song "Imagine" encourages us to imagine there is no heaven or hell. Instead, we should embrace the need to live for today. The song was a big hit when it was released and is now recognized as one of the greatest rock/pop songs of all time. The lyrics summed up the mood of the post-1960s era, a time in which people were questioning religious claims and traditional morality.

Forty years later, many evangelicals are now following Lennon's advice. We are told that the gospel is not really about the afterlife. The gospel answers much bigger questions than a person's eternal state. It's all about life today—not so much about tomorrow.

Unfortunately, the "big gospel" championed by some segments of evangelicalism isn't big enough to include the full picture. Of course we should see the gospel as speaking to life today. And yes, the gospel is not only about going to heaven when we die. But we must take care that, in our efforts to enlarge our vision of the gospel, we hold together *all* the components of the gospel story in which the gospel announcement makes sense.

Judgment Day

The Apostle's Creed tells us that Christ will come again to judge the living and the dead. Expounding on this line, the Heidelberg Catechism asks, "Why does this knowledge bring comfort?" Upon first glance, this seems like a strange question. "Jesus is coming back to *judge,*" we say. So take *comfort*?

I don't know what you think of when you hear the words "Judgment Day," but it sounds dreadful to me. My mind races to "end of the world" movies that describe an apocalypse of epic proportions. And even when I remember that I need to let the Bible—not Hollywood—shape my understanding of judgment, I find many reasons to be terrified. Just think: *God's holy and righteous judgment being poured out on all that is wrong with us and the world.* Yikes!

But there is something comforting about God's judgment. Something that the writers of the Catechism recognize as integral to the gospel story. It's something we don't want to miss.

Judgment and Justice

Our two-year-old daughter is just now learning to talk, and we are just now learning to understand her! Whenever she bumps her head on the table or gets her fingers caught in a drawer, she cries as she explains to us what happened. My wife and I know that she'll calm down faster if we bang on the table or pound the drawer. "Bad table!" "Bad drawer!" I'm not sure why this brings our daughter comfort. It doesn't make her pain go away more quickly. We don't do it because the inanimate object is guilty of anything. No . . . I believe our daughter is consoled because, in her little brain, she senses that justice (however strange in this case) has somehow been served.

Even as children, we possess an innate sense of right and wrong. Humans are united by a desire for justice. We realize that that life isn't fair. And yet for some reason, we also think it *should* be fair. The Bible teaches that life isn't fair *now*, and yet Scripture still points to a day when wrongs will be righted and justice will be served. God will straighten things out once and for all.

That's why the idea of Christ's return in judgment brings comfort. To those who suffer at the hands of the unjust, it is comforting to hold on to the promise that one day all will be made right. This upside-down, crazy world will not go on in its current state forever. God will execute justice. The righteousness of God will be evident for all to see, and the knowledge of the Lord will flood the earth as the waters cover the sea.

But there is also a scary side to this idea of a world of perfect justice. Just think: If God were to return and purge the world of evil, what would happen to us? Would we be able to inhabit a perfect world? What happens when we realize that we are part of the problem, not just the ones longing for a solution?

When we take our place within the cosmic story of redemption, we come to realize that we are more than passive victims of evil's consequences. We are evil insurrectionists, rebels against the good and loving authority of God our Creator.

The author Alexandyr Solzhenitsyn, who suffered at the hands of the communists in Russia, put it well: "Gradually it was disclosed to me that the line separating good and evil passes not through states, nor between classes, nor between political parties either—but right through every human heart—and through all human hearts."[1] We thirst for justice, but once we consider the fairness of God, we quickly discover that Christ's return can only be good news if we have found mercy in God's sight.

The Judgmentless Gospel

The temptation in our day and age is to let the last part of the Apostle's Creed slip by unnoticed. Many evangelicals talk a lot about justice and very little about judgment. Justice here and now is a popular subject. Judgment there and then? Not so much.

But justice and judgment are two sides to the same coin. You cannot have perfect justice without judgment. God cannot make things right without declaring certain things wrong. It's the judgment of God that leads to a perfectly just world. Try to take one without the other and you lose the good news.

The judgmentless gospel distorts a major part of the gospel story—the end. And if you've ever heard a good story, you know that once you change the ending, you alter everything.

One of Alfred Hitchcock's most acclaimed movies is *Vertigo*, which begins as a mystery and then turns into a story about murder and a case of double identity. Originally, the final scene of the 1958 film was to show two of the main characters listening to a radio report that the man who masterminded the murder had been found and arrested. But Hitchcock decided that the ending was unnecessary and instead finished the film in a much more ambivalent manner that left the viewer wondering if justice was ever served.[2] *Vertigo* is a terrific film, but it leaves you without a sense of resolution. Justice never takes place.

Neglecting or denying the idea of God as Judge changes the story. Without judgment, sin becomes less serious. The implications of human rebellion are downplayed. No longer is human sin considered cosmic treason against our Creator, and the offer of forgiveness loses its power. If there is no eternal judgment, just what do we need to be saved from?

So the judgmentless gospel alters the gospel story, diminishes the need for the gospel announcement, and eventually changes the make-up of the gospel community as well. When we fail to see God in His role as Judge, we lose our distinctiveness. Our efforts to minimize boundaries between who is "inside" and "outside" the kingdom dilute the power of our witness. Do you see how all three legs of the stool are affected by this one counterfeit?

The Forms of the Judgmentless Gospel

The judgmentless gospel shows up in many forms. Sometimes the forms are scholarly presentations of why there is no judgment or why—if there is—we shouldn't worry too much about it. Other times, the forms show up in the way Christians soften the idea. We might call these forms "judgment-lite." Here are some ways that we downplay judgment.

"Everybody is going to heaven."

Universalism is the belief that, in the end, every human being will be saved. It was first proposed by Origen, an early theologian. The church widely rejected this view because of the number of Bible passages that contradict it.

Many people today adopt a modified universalism based upon a common perception that just about everyone is going to heaven. There may be a few horrible people who wind up facing eternal judgment, but hell is the exception and heaven the norm. On the contrary, the biblical portrait shows us *all* on the road to eternal condemnation until God intervenes in our plight and rescues us.

Strangely, some Christians still affirm the importance (even necessity) of conversion for salvation but act as if most everyone is probably okay with God. Not too long ago, an elderly Christian invited me to lunch. During our time together, he confided in me that he had serious doubts about the existence of hell. I could tell from our conversation that he was not rejecting the idea of hell out of a rebellious spirit or an aversion to biblical authority. He simply couldn't understand why hell was necessary for Christianity. My question to him was: "Do you believe in justice?" He had never considered the idea of hell from this angle. For him, the thought of hell was naturally *unjust,* until he considered the need for wrongs to be righted and our sin against God to be punished.

I suspect that many Christians are like that man. On paper and in public, they would affirm that one must repent and believe in Jesus for salvation. But deep down, they are practical universalists, acting as if everyone and everything will turn out okay in the end.

"The afterlife is not as important as the mission life."

It has become popular to point out how evangelicals have overemphasized one's eternal destiny. It is said that our focus on the afterlife (heaven and hell) has led to a stunted discipleship that leaves little room for personal transformation today. The solution to this problem is to make clear that the Bible speaks about life *here and now* and not simply about heaven and hell in the future.

On one level, this critique is valid. Growing up in evangelical churches, I sensed every mention of the Christian life aimed at a one-time decision in which one's eternity was resolved. The goal of Christianity was to go to heaven with as many people as you can.

Yet the biblical portrait of salvation is much richer than simply thrusting the images of heaven and hell at people and saying, "Choose!" Ultimate salvation in the New Testament is not about us going to heaven, but about heaven coming down to earth. (That's one reason we pray, "Your kingdom come . . . on earth as in heaven.") New heavens and new earth with resurrected bodies in a New Jerusalem sound much more glorious than the disembodied intermediate state between death and the resurrection.

True, at times evangelicals have skewed the biblical portrait by condensing the glorious gospel story into little more than making a reservation for heavenly accommodations after death. But in newer gospel presentations, the afterlife often disappears altogether. Or maybe heaven remains, but not the notion of eternal judgment. What's more, the idea of "mission" becomes so broad that it includes just about every good thing a Christian does. Evangelism is downplayed, and the urgency of calling people to repentance dissipates.

I fear that evangelical distaste for the heaven/hell conversation has less to do with the Bible and more to do with the current cultural climate. People today are far less likely to be concerned with eternity. Many people go through much of their lives without considering death, much less judgment.

But who determines relevancy? If a nuclear attack in a major city killed hundreds of thousands of people and we were brought face to face with the possibility of immediate death, would the afterlife question suddenly become relevant again? Would it then be appropriate to shift back from the emphasis on "mission life" to "afterlife"?

It's true that our eternal destiny is not the only important aspect of Christian evangelism or discipleship. But eternity *is* important. Making the Bible only about God's kingdom on earth here and now does justice to one part of the picture, but flattens out the bigger picture of eventual cosmic restoration under the reign of King Jesus—a restoration that also includes judgment of all that remains in a state of rebellion against Him.

"God doesn't send anyone to hell. People choose to go there." This form of the counterfeit is actually very close to getting it right. It is true that those who reject God in this life will find that they are separated from His love after their death. C. S. Lewis gave us the imaginative example of hell with the doors locked on the inside.[3] It's not that people *couldn't* get out, but that they wouldn't want to. They would rather remain in their man-made prison of selfishness than submit to the loving pursuit of God their creator.

When looking at hell from this angle, it is said that God doesn't send people to hell. People choose to go there themselves. They would rather have hell than God. This is close to the biblical truth. Those who choose their sin instead of Christ are indeed choosing the consequence of eternal perdition.

But though it's true that condemnation is the consequence of our sinful choices on earth, it's not enough to speak of hell as *merely* consequential. There are too many biblical passages that describe God as actively judging sinners. Jesus himself will say to the unrighteous: "I never knew you! depart from me" (Matthew 7:23). Jesus told parables that portray God casting people into the outer darkness, where there is weeping and gnashing of teeth. His story of Lazarus and the rich man shows the rich man in agony. Even if the rich man doesn't ask to be delivered, it's clear that he desires relief. It's hard to make the case that he *wants* hell.

The frightening truth that we see in Scripture is that eternal condemnation is not the absence of God, but the presence of God in His wrath. Surely this view of judgment is unpopular and has negative connotations. It may be hard to stomach. But if Christianity is true, we should expect it to confront our presuppositions and views at several points. This may be the place it hits us Westerners the hardest. In trying to make sense of the biblical portrait of eternal judgment, we are left with no other choice. As glorious and majestic as the New Testament portrayal of resurrection and new creation is, so horrific and terrifying is its portrayal of God's wrath against sinners outside of Christ.

"God looks at your heart."

Preachers on television sometimes use the phrase, "Well, God knows the heart . . . " when asked about Jesus being the only way to God. The assumption is that because God can look deep down into the human heart and see the goodness of each person, He might give us a pass.

But when we consider what the Scriptures say about human nature, "God looks at my heart" is not good news at all. Just think: God looks into your heart and knows *everything* about you. Our hearts devise wicked schemes that our hands never carry out.[4] Knowing that God looks at my heart is scary, not comforting.

This form of the counterfeit is appealing because many believe that deep down, humans are basically good people who simply have gone astray. And people who sincerely seek God will be okay in the end, since God will look into their hearts.

But this brings up a bigger, more fundamental question: Who determines what is good? If we fail to answer *this* question, we can simply adopt the world's standard of "goodness" and apply it uncritically to the people around us. It is true that a good Buddhist, a good Muslim, and a good Hindu will all go to heaven, if by "good" we mean what Scripture teaches—absolute moral perfection. The problem is not that good people do not go to heaven. The problem is there are no good people.

SPOTTING THE COUNTERFEIT

the judgmentless gospel

STORY	ANNOUNCEMENT	COMMUNITY
Restoration is more about God's goodness than His judgment of evil or His response to rebellious humanity.	Jesus' death is more about defeating humanity's enemies (death, sin, Satan) than the need for God's wrath to be averted by His sacrifice.	The boundaries between the church and the world are blurred in a way that makes personal evangelism less urgent and unnecessary.

Why Is This Counterfeit Attractive?

We have looked at some ways that we try to soften the idea of judgment in the Bible. The judgmentless gospel comes in many forms. Some of the minor forms still contain the notion of judgment, although this judgment might be called "judgment-lite." Why is the judgmentless gospel so attractive today? There are several reasons:

It removes an emotional barrier to Christianity.

Let's face it. One reason we are attracted to this counterfeit is because it helps us get past a significant emotional barrier to sharing our faith. If we remove the obstacle and offense of eternal judgment, we will be in a better position to make Christianity more palatable to a society that has no room for judgment in its understanding of God.

Unfortunately, when we downplay or deny judgment, we lose one of the reasons to share our faith in the first place. Our desire to remove the obstacle actually removes the urgency.

It eases our conscience.

Another reason this counterfeit is attractive is that it eases our conscience when we fail to evangelize. It would take a load off my shoulders to affirm, along with Origen, that all will eventually be saved, including the devil. But the Bible doesn't let me go down that road. Adopting the counterfeit also helps us deal emotionally with the fact that we have unsaved friends and family members who have died. We don't want to imagine that Grandpa may be in hell. Downplaying judgment helps us cope.

It keeps us from having to come face to face with our own evil.

Most of us in the West have been shielded from the atrocities of humanity. If we were to have experienced Cambodia's killing fields or Auschwitz or Rwanda, we might be more concerned about justice. Os Guinness quotes Winston Churchill as saying that the evidence that God exists was "the existence of Lenin and Trotsky, for whom a hell was needed."[5]

Once we admit that justice is necessary, we open the door for our own sins to be dealt with. Perhaps this counterfeit is attractive because there is a part of us that would like to suppress justice rather than admit justice and thus indict ourselves.

Countering the Counterfeit

The judgmentless gospel may be the most attractive counterfeit being proposed today. The entire tide of our culture is turning toward a type of pluralism that would deny the reality (and even the need) for divine justice. Here are some ways we can keep from falling for these forms of the judgmentless gospel:

Recognize the good news of judgment.

You may be wondering: *How can judgment be good news?* Good question. The answer goes back to our love for justice. Once we understand God's judgment as putting an end to all that is wrong with the world (war, famine, disease, etc.), then we can understand why even the apostle Paul viewed judgment as part of his gospel. In Romans 2, he writes: "They show that the work of the law is written on their hearts, while their conscience also bears witness, and their conflicting thoughts accuse or even excuse them on that day when, *according to my gospel*, God judges the secrets of men by Christ Jesus" (Romans 2:15–16, emphasis added). According to the gospel, God will judge humanity.

The Old Testament also sees God's judgment as good news. Look at Psalm 96:

> Worship the Lord in the splendor of holiness; tremble before him, all the earth! Say among the nations, "The Lord reigns! Yes, the world is established; it shall never be moved; *he will judge the peoples with equity*." Let the heavens be glad, and let the earth rejoice; let the sea roar, and all that fills it; let the field exult, and everything in it! Then shall all the trees of the forest sing for joy

before the Lord, *for he comes, for he comes to judge the earth. He will judge the world in righteousness, and the peoples in his faithfulness.* (vv. 9–13, emphasis added)

Apparently the writers of our Bible had no problem with celebrating judgment as good news. The idea of Jesus coming to judge the living and the dead was cause not only for comfort (as the Heidelberg Catechism states), but also for celebration.

Take away the notion of judgment, and you rob Christianity of any hope of satisfying our longing for justice, a longing built into us by our just and wise God. The judgmentless gospel fails to deal with the problem of evil and the detrimental way that we humans treat each other (and by extension, God). Once we take away judgment, we lose the gravity of our sin. Once we lose sight of our sinfulness, we short-circuit our experience of the powerful gratitude that comes from receiving grace.

See how judgment demonstrates the holy love of God.

God is not a bipolar deity—one side wrathful and angry, the other loving and merciful. Love is His essential attribute, but this love is not like the sentimental love we think of today. God's love is holy. It is jealous. The wrath of God is based in His love. The idea of biblical judgment not only assures us of future justice. It also gives us a clearer picture of the love of God.

Think of a loving father who has a son and daughter. If someone were to kidnap and abuse that father's children, what kind of love would the father have if he felt no anger? No wrath? Or let's say that a son and daughter are rebelling against their father's authority and destroying their lives. If the father loves his son and daughter, his anger and wrath toward their sinful behavior is based in his love for them and his desire for their best.

What the judgmentless gospel leaves us with is a one-dimensional God—a sappy, sanitized deity that we can easily manage. He nods and winks at our behavior, much like a kind, elderly man who is not seriously invested in our lives. But the evil of our world is much too serious for us to view God as a pandering papa.

The picture of God in the Bible is much more satisfying. He is angry *because* He is love. He looks at the world and sees the trafficking of innocent girls, the destructive use of drugs, the genocidal atrocities in Africa, the terrorist attacks that keep people in perpetual fear, and He—out of love for the creation that reflects Him as creator—is rightfully and gloriously angry. Real love always wants the best for the beloved.[6]

The god who is *truly* scary is not the wrathful God of the Bible, but the god of the judgmentless gospel, who closes his eyes to the evil of this world, shrugs his shoulders, and ignores it in the name of "love." What kind of "love" is this? A god who is never angered at sin and who lets evil go by unpunished is not worthy of worship. The problem isn't that the judgmentless God is too loving; it's that he's not loving enough.

> GOD IS ANGRY ~~BECAUSE~~ HE IS LOVE. REAL LOVE ALWAYS WANTS THE BEST FOR THE BELOVED.

In Exodus, God reveals Himself to Moses as "the Lord, a God merciful and gracious, slow to anger, and abounding in steadfast love and faithfulness, keeping steadfast love to thousands, forgiving iniquity, transgression and sin." And then he adds, "But [He] will by no means clear the guilty" (34:6–7). In other words, God's mercy and compassion is not divorced from his justice. A god without judgment is "a god who simply hides sin—or even hides *from* sin—rather than confronting it and destroying it. It makes him a moral coward."[7]

Eternal judgment only makes sense if we understand that we live in a good world created by a loving God. Sin has unleashed destruction and heartache into the world. That is why creation is groaning for redemption and judgment, the time when the purging fire will lay bare everything in this world that defaces it and leave us with room for God's presence to fill it once again.

Remember the personal nature of our sin.

God hates sin because of what it does to us. He hates sin because of what it does to His good creation. He rages against sin because of His great love for His children. But it's not enough to say that God will judge sin and restore creation *for our benefit.* This is a step in the right direction, but it leaves out a crucial component of sin and judgment. God is wrathful toward sin—not only because of what it does to us, but because of what it does to *Him.* It dishonors His name.

When we depersonalize God's judgment and make it merely negative consequences (the outworking of sinful actions), we wind up with a lopsided view of sin. Sin is not merely bad *for us.* All the sins we commit against one another are ultimately against God.

We see this truth throughout Scripture. When Joseph is tempted by Potiphar's wife, he refuses to go to bed with her because it would be a great sin against Potiphar *and against God.* Joseph realizes that sinning against his master, in effect stabbing him in the back, would also be plunging a dagger into the heart of God. He realizes that sin, even sin against other humans, is directed toward God.

Likewise, we see King David succumb to temptation when he lusts after Bathsheba. After he sleeps with her, he tries to cover up the pregnancy and ends up having her husband, Uriah, killed. He lies and finagles a way to keep his sin covered, implicating even his faithful army commanders. His sin affects multiple people.

Yet David's prayer of confession contains this line: "Against you, and you *only,* have I sinned" (Psalm 51:4, emphasis added). How can this be true? The story shows him sinning against many people. Yet in his confession he claims that his sin is against God alone. Why? Because all sin is ultimately a replay of Adam and

Eve's very personal betrayal and rejection of God Himself.

Why is it necessary that we make judgment personal? Because our sin is personal. It is directed to God and must be dealt with personally.

Find comfort in knowing that good will be vindicated in the end.

We can learn a lot from the psalms. All the emotions one feels as a Christian are contained in these hymns of praise and lament to God. At times, one soars with

ALL SIN IS ULTIMATELY A REPLAY OF ADAM AND EVE'S VERY PERSONAL REJECTION OF GOD.

the psalmist to the highest heights of praise and exaltation. Other times, one sinks with the psalmist to the lowest depths of despair, wondering if God is in control, and if so, what He is doing.

There are also psalms that are called "imprecatory." The psalmist calls down judgment on his enemies. He asks God to act decisively in his favor and judge who is right and who is wrong. I have heard a number of explanations for these psalms. Most flatten them out, spiritualize them, disregard them as irrelevant for New Testament times, or simply ignore them.

But people in other parts of the world find comfort in these psalms. Why? These believers have seen evil face to face. They have true enemies. They are subject to countless atrocities. When you suffer at the hands of others, when your faith costs something, when you watch loved ones tortured for their faith and you are at the hands of merciless injustice, then it makes sense to cry out, "O Sovereign Lord, holy and true, how long before you will judge and avenge our blood on those who dwell on the earth?" (Revelation 6:10). When going to church brings you into contact with secret police who threaten and beat you, then you long for deliverance and justice.

Job says, "From out of the city the dying groan, and the soul of the wounded cries for help; yet God charges no one with wrong" (Job 24:12). Job yearns for justice, for God to vindicate righteous behavior and punish wicked behavior. "Judgment— the sovereign declaration that *this* is good and to be upheld and vindicated, and *that* is evil and to be condemned—is the only alternative to chaos."[8]

It puzzles me that so many people seem to be angry with God for allowing evil and suffering to exist in this world, and yet they are also angry with the idea of God as Judge. You can't have it both ways. If you expect God to do something about the evil in this world, then you want God to judge.

Recognize that the concept of judgment is good for society.
We believe in judgment because we find the concept clearly taught within the Bible. Nevertheless, judgment is also good news for society. Dinesh D'Souza makes a powerful case for an afterlife—including the possibility of judgment—and he appeals to the idea that societies function better when there is the expectation of divine judgment after death.[9]

Take a Communist regime like Nicolae Ceausescu's Romania. My wife grew up in this environment, and she witnessed firsthand the injustices that took place there. Ceausescu was an avowed atheist who had no tolerance for people who believed in God. Because he had no fear of what might occur after death, he could live in luxury while systematically starving his people. Without any fear of standing before his Maker, Ceausescu was able to justify any selfish craving that he had.

Ultimately, taking away the idea of judgment "secretly nourishes violence," Miroslav Volf, another Eastern European writes. "If I don't believe that there is a God who will eventually put all things right, I *will* take up the sword and will be sucked into the endless vortex of retaliation."[10]

Admit your own sin and that you deserve to be judged.
The reason this counterfeit is especially attractive is because it keeps us from coming face to face with our own sins. We are good at spotting evil in the world, while remaining blind to the evil in our own hearts. The best way to counter the judgmentless gospel is to humble ourselves by admitting our own sin and that we too deserve eternal condemnation.

In *They Thought They Were Free,* Milton Mayer, a Jewish journalist, documents a series of interviews with average Germans who went along with the Nazi atrocities during World War II. Mayer's book attempts to show how people in a civilized country could be complicit in such terrible crimes. As the narrative progresses, Mayer is disgusted by the hypocrisy of the Germans who continue to justify their actions:

> What we don't like, what I don't like, is the hypocrisy of these people. I want to hear them confess. That they, or some of their countrymen and their country's government, violated the precepts of Christian, civilized, lawful life was bad enough; that they won't see it, or say it, is what really rowels. . . . I want them to say, "I knew and I know that it was all un-Christian, uncivilized, unlawful, and in my love of evil I pretended it wasn't. I plead every German guilty of a life of hypocrisy, above all, myself. I am rotten."

But as Mayer probes deeper into his desire for justice, he comes face to face with his own sinful desire for control:

> I want my friends not just to feel bad and confess it, but to have been bad and to be bad now and confess it. I want them to constitute themselves an inferior race, self-abased, so that I, in the magnanimity becoming to the superior, having sat in calumnious judgment on them, may choose to let them live on in public

shame and in private torment. I want to be God, not alone in power but in righteousness and in mercy; and Nazism crushed is my chance. But I am not God.[11]

When we stand before the God of the Bible, we are frightened by the perfect righteousness we see. Yet we are also astounded by the grace of God shown to us in Jesus Christ. It's not divine judgment that is so radical; it's divine favor!

Larry King, who often asks Christian preachers about Jesus being the only way to God, also asks them about the murderer who trusts Christ. Does he get off the hook? Can a murderer enter heaven? The idea that a criminal could go free is astounding, and indeed it is . . . but God has acted in a way that upholds justice and lavishes grace at the same time.

There is hope for rebels who desire justice and yet don't want to suffer. We see justice and mercy most clearly in the cross of Jesus Christ. The cross of Christ vindicates God's name. All of us who have put our faith in Jesus Christ are likewise vindicated, "declared righteous" because we are united to Christ—the Righteous One.

God the Judge has promised to completely wipe out the evil of the world. And yet, He loves us. In His grace, He is the righteous judge and the gracious redeemer. His wrath toward evil is poured out upon His only Son on the cross. Justice and mercy are not at war with one another. They meet at the cross. And we can find both judgment and mercy as good news. We need only recognize our guilt in light of God's holiness and then bask in forgiveness in light of God's grace.

Scripture Truths

ON THE JUSTICE OF GOD: *Psalm 11:7; Psalm 33:5; Psalm 89:14; Psalm 97:12*

ON LONGING TO BE FOUND RIGHTEOUS: *Psalm 7:10; Psalm 31:1; Psalm 65:5; Psalm 143:11; Psalm 35:24*

ON THE REALITY OF ETERNAL JUDGMENT: *Matthew 7:23; 25:31–46; Mark 9:42–48; Luke 16:19–31; 2 Thessalonians 1:5–10; Revelation 14*

ON JUDGMENT AS GOOD NEWS AND THE DESIRE FOR JUSTICE: *Job 24; Psalm 96; Romans 2:15–16; Revelation 6:10*

ON THE HOLINESS OF GOD'S LOVE: *Exodus 33:7–34:9*

ON THE PERSONAL NATURE OF OUR SIN: *Genesis 3; 39:9; Psalm 51:4*

ON BEING JUSTIFIED BY THE JUST JUDGE: *Romans 3:21–31*

PART 2

ANNOUNCEMENT

The Truth
the gospel announcement

A Counterfeit
the moralistic gospel

A Counterfeit
the quietist gospel

A single act of forgiveness can change everything.

– The Tale of Despereaux

the gospel announcement

WE THOUGHT we were ready. Baby crib? Check. Closet full of baby clothes? Check. Diapers and diaper bag? Check. We'd read the books and done our homework. Frankly, my wife and I were worn out and ready for our first child to make his appearance. A few days before the birth, I made an offhand remark: "I can't wait for the baby to get here so things can settle down." Silly comment. After you have a child, there is no "settling down." Everything changes. There is only a "new normal."

The same was true when our second child came along. I had spent all day writing and was looking forward to a quiet evening at home. When my wife's water broke, our plans changed. All we could do was react! We packed our bags, hurried our son over to a friend's house, and then got in the car and rushed to the hospital.

It's interesting that several of the apostles used "new birth" as a metaphor when speaking of what takes place when someone believes the gospel. The gospel announcement brings about new birth because it is about a new reality. The announcement that Jesus Christ has been raised from the dead alters the landscape forever. Once we truly grasp the nature of the gospel announcement, there is no going back. There is no "settling down." Like a new birth in a human family, new spiritual birth shatters all normalcy. Everything changes. New creation has begun!

How the Gospel Announcement Fits into the Gospel Story

The gospel is like a three-legged stool. We have a *story*, an *announcement*, and a *community*. We have already looked at the basic structure of the gospel story, the grand narrative that tells the story of our world from creation to new creation. The reason we begin with the gospel story is because the good news needs context in order to make sense.

Let's imagine that I were to make an announcement out of the blue: "The basement is safe!" The announcement itself could mean any number of things. Maybe the basement had structural damage and had been under construction for awhile. Maybe there's a killer on the loose, and the police have just checked the basement and announced it is secure.

But let's say that I tell you the backstory first: A tornado is coming, destroying everything in its path. There's no place to run, but "the basement is safe!" Suddenly, a puzzling piece of news becomes very good indeed. You rush to the basement where you remain until the storm passes by.

The same is true of the gospel announcement. Graeme Goldsworthy has defined the announcement this way: "The gospel is the word about Jesus Christ and what He did for us in order to restore us to a right relationship with God."[1] We need the gospel story in order to know why we need a right relationship with God. We need the gospel announcement in order to know how to escape the storm of God's wrath. You can't tell the gospel story without making the announcement of good news; neither can you properly make the announcement without telling the story.

Gospel Announcement and Personal Testimony

Before we look at the specifics of the gospel announcement, we need to make sure that we are clear on *who* the good news is about. Many believe that the best way to proclaim the gospel is to share your personal testimony because no one can argue with your personal experience. Tell others about your life before you knew Christ, how you came to know Christ, and what your life is like now. Then tell them that the same experience can happen to them too.

Personal testimonies can be effective as a witness to God's power in salvation. The Samaritan woman at the well told what Jesus did for her. The blind man in John 9 gave his testimony too. Saul—later Paul—tells of his conversion multiple times in Acts.

But the story of how God has changed *you* is not the gospel. Your life transformation testifies to the power of the gospel, but it is not the good news. If you share your personal story and yet do not tell the story of Jesus Christ—specifically His life, death, and resurrection—you are not proclaiming the gospel announcement.

The very reason that personal testimonies are appealing ("no one can argue with it!") is the reason such testimonies are insufficient. The gospel announcement is centered on Christ and His work in reconciling the world to God, not you and your life change.

This announcement is rooted in history. Goldsworthy writes: "The gospel is the event (or the proclamation of that event) of Jesus Christ that begins with his incarnation and earthly life, and concludes with his death, resurrection and ascension to the right hand of the Father."[2]

We must not confuse aspects of the biblical story or theological truths surrounding the gospel with the gospel itself. "If something is not what God did in and through the historical Jesus two thousand years ago, it is not the gospel. Thus Christians cannot 'live the gospel,' as they are often exhorted to do. They can only believe it, proclaim it, and seek to live consistently with it. Only Jesus lived (and died) the gospel. It is a once-for-all finished and perfect event done for us by another."[3]

How can we briefly outline this gospel announcement of Jesus Christ? There are a number of ways, but four main headings are helpful. We will look at the good news of Christ's life, Christ's death, Christ's resurrection, and Christ's exaltation as Lord. This announcement then provokes a response from us—repentance and faith.

The Life of Jesus

The creeds of the early church are like guardrails that keep us on the right track, making sure that we affirm the essential truths of Christianity. But they are not infallible. Sometimes they overemphasize some truths and underemphasize others.

Take the Apostle's Creed, for example. We confess that "Jesus was conceived by the power of the Holy Spirit and born of the Virgin Mary. He suffered under Pontius Pilate, was crucified . . . " What's missing here? Christ's life! We jump from the manger to the cross.

Many of us know very well why Jesus had to die; fewer know why He had to live. What are all the miracles about? Why did He tell such puzzling stories? Why the confrontations with religious leaders? Why the unattainable ethical commands? Obviously, God wanted us to know about Jesus' life. Otherwise, we wouldn't have the four Gospels.

Significantly, the early church labeled Matthew, Mark, Luke, and John as "Gospels" and not the "letters of the apostles." Of course, the gospel announcement pulsates through the apostolic letters as the writers unpack and interpret Christ's life and death.

But the four biographies of Jesus are labeled "Gospels" because—at some level—the story of Jesus is the "good news." Jesus doesn't just *bring* us good news. He *is* the good news—God's revelation to us. The story of God becoming human is at the heart of the gospel announcement.

The Arrival of God's Kingdom

The heartbeat of all of Jesus' preaching was the kingdom of God. Put simply, the kingdom of God is the reign of God. It's God working to fix this world and make everything right, pushing back the effects of our rebellion and offering us His forgiveness. Jesus comes to establish this reign. His life shouts, "God is fulfilling His promises! God is acting on behalf of His people! God is making all things new!" And the startling claim that accompanies this message is, "God is doing all of this *through Me!*" Jesus is the Messiah King, the divine Son of God who has come to earth as a servant and through whom God is restoring His world.

C. S. Lewis captured this theme in *The Lion, the Witch and the Wardrobe.* The world of Narnia is suffering under the terrible curse of the White Witch. It is always winter, but never Christmas. But once the lion Aslan, the rightful king of Narnia, returns to his world, everything begins to change. "Aslan is on the move!" Then Father Christmas arrives, handing out presents and wishing all a merry Christmas. The long winter of Narnia is coming to an end. The snow begins to melt. Flowers begin to bloom. The signs of spring appear, announcing that the King is returning to restore his world.[4]

In a similar way, Jesus' life demonstrates the arrival of God's kingdom. When a furious tempest threatens to overturn the disciples' boat, Jesus calms the storm. The effects of the curse on the created order are temporarily removed as He takes control.

When people are blind and lame, Jesus restores their sight and their mobility. They are healed because in God's kingdom, wholeness—not sickness—is the rule.

When Jesus feeds people in the wilderness, He is demonstrating that in God's kingdom, no one goes hungry.

When Jesus raises people from the dead, He is saying that even death itself is no match for the kingdom of God. Over and over again, in His actions and words, Jesus shows us who He is (God in human flesh) and what His kingdom is like.

Our Perfect Righteousness

As Jesus brings the kingdom of God, He also lives in a way that meets every requirement for taking part in His kingdom. Christ not only died for us, He *lived* for us. He fulfills God's intention for humanity by being perfectly faithful to his Father's will.

The Gospel writers tell the story of Jesus in a way that highlights Christ's fulfillment of God's law in our place. The Gospel writers show us that Jesus succeeds where Adam failed. Jesus succeeds where Israel failed. And—glory to God!—Jesus succeeds where you and I fail. Because Adam sinned, we are guilty before God. Because Christ obeyed, we are declared righteous in God's sight.

The Forgiveness of Sins and Restoration of Shalom

The arrival of God's kingdom and the sinless life of Jesus are integral parts of the gospel announcement. But Christ's work is primarily to restore us to God and thereby to restore the shalom that our sin shattered. Have you ever noticed how many times Jesus told the people He healed to "go in peace"? More than a generic blessing, this pronouncement of shalom is the direct result of having one's sin forgiven. In Luke 7, for example, Jesus tells a woman of disrepute, "Your sins are forgiven." Then he says, "Your faith has saved you; go in peace!" See the progression? Forgiveness of sins pronounced, faith exercised, shalom restored.

Some evangelicals deemphasize the kingdom of God, focusing most of their attention on the need to be forgiven. Other evangelicals emphasize the kingdom and make forgiveness to be a very small part of God's plan to restore the world. But the Gospel writers hold these two concepts together. For God's world to be put back together, humans must be forgiven and made right with God. Only once we are reconciled to our King can we begin to reflect His glory into creation in a way that restores shalom.

The classic story *The Tale of Despereaux* by Kate DiCamillo, tells the story of a once-joyous town that is overcome with grief. The sun stops shining. The clouds never give rain. The joy of the town (soup) is banned. Hurt on top of hurt leads to bitterness, despair, and more pain. The climax of the movie takes place with one pronouncement of forgiveness. The main characters begin to grant forgiveness to one another.

Suddenly, everything changes. The sun comes back out. Soup is back on the stove. The clouds start giving rain again. In the story, cosmic restoration follows forgiveness.[5] The gospel announcement says the same. Forgiveness leads to restoration.

The Death of Jesus

People who have given their lives for what they believe inspire us. Martyrs like Martin Luther King, Jr., Abraham Lincoln, and William Wallace believed in their causes and went to the grave sounding the trumpet.

But we don't glory in the deaths of these men. There's no celebration of Abraham Lincoln's assassination. Neither do we revel in the details of how the patriot William Wallace was killed. Their deaths are the final chapter in a story of their lives; martyrdom is the end of their story.

Jesus is different. We focus intently on the events surrounding His execution. The Gospel of Mark gives such a disproportionate amount of attention to Christ's death that it has been called "a passion narrative with an extended introduction." Everything in Jesus' life is a journey toward the cross, and six out of Mark's sixteen chapters are about the days leading up to Jesus' crucifixion.

The other Gospel writers focus on Christ's death too. One of Luke's longest sections records Jesus' journey to Jerusalem, in which he "set his face" toward David's city. The persistent idea in some circles that the Gospel writers were interested in Jesus' kingdom message and not His atoning death is a myth. Martin Luther was right: "No theology is genuinely Christian which does not arise from and focus on the cross."[6]

The Atoning King

The kingdom of God turns upside down the notions of kingship in this world. It is through the death of Christ that we see the heart of God. Jesus came to reign, and His throne was a splintery cross. The disciples asked for seats next to Jesus in His glory, but they abandoned Him once He was lifted up on the cross between two rebels. Christ's shameful death was His glory.

THE ATONEMENT IS AT THE HEART OF WHO GOD IS AND WHAT HE HAS DONE FOR US.

Theologians debate the significance of Christ's death on the cross. At stake is the nature of the atonement, the idea of Christ dying as a sacrifice for our sins. Some writers believe that evangelicals have emphasized Christ dying as our substitute to the point that we have excluded other important metaphors. Others pit these theories against one another. (Interestingly, a recent proposal advocates a "kaleidoscopic view" that is open to all theories, except apparently the substitutionary view.)

The Bible doesn't pit atonement theories against one another. It presents Christ's sacrifice like a multifaceted diamond. What Christ accomplished on the cross is so massive, and the window into the heart of God is so big that no *one* explanation or description of the atonement can tell the whole story. Because the atonement is at the heart of who God is and what He has done for us, we can never fully exhaust the riches that flow from this event. But recognizing our inability to mine all the theological treasures represented in the cross of Christ should not keep us from pondering the beautiful truth of this event.

Paul says the gospel is the news that Jesus, the Messiah-King, "died *for our sins* in accordance with the Scriptures" (1 Corinthians 15:3, emphasis added). Under this one truth all the other atonement theories find their place. The heart of the atonement is that Christ bore the wrath of God in our place, taking upon Himself the punishment that our sin deserved.

Each of the other atonement theories shines light on this truth from different angles. The *Christus victor* model tells us that Jesus won the battle against Satan, sin, and death *in our place*. The ransom theory uses a marketplace analogy that says Christ paid for our sins; he made the purchase *in our place*. The recapitulation theory says that Christ undid the curse of Adam *in our place*.

Notice the common thread? Substitution.[7] *Christ died for our sins in accordance with the Scriptures.* At the heart of the atonement is the idea that Christ has substituted Himself for us. He has taken upon Himself the punishment for our sins. Together these various images give us a better understanding of Christ's substitutionary death, enhancing (not supplanting) this truth.

God with Us

In November 2008, Mumbai, the largest city in India, became the target of a series of coordinated terrorist attacks that killed 173 people. Two of the victims were from New York—a Jewish Rabbi and his wife, both in their late twenties. Kashmiri militants entered the rabbi's home and slaughtered him and his wife. The couple's nanny found their two-year-old son, Moshe, sitting in a pool of his parents' blood.

When the memorial service took place in Brooklyn, New

York, the two-year-old boy cried out for his slain parents. "Ima! Abba!" he said, using the Hebrew words for mother and father. "Ima! Abba!" he moaned. Little Moshe's mournful wail echoed through the synagogue, drowning out the voices of the hundreds of people grieving his parents' death.

An inconsolable two-year-old, crying out for his dead parents. My heart wells up with the question, *Why?* Why does God allow this kind of pain? Why is the world such a messed-up, broken place?

How do we make sense of the evil that exists in a world of such beauty? What would it be like to witness the changing of the seasons from behind the barbed wire of a concentration camp? How does a Holocaust victim admire a glorious sunset when it serves as the backdrop for smoke rising to the sky, smoke coming from piles of burning bodies of men, women, and children?

BECAUSE OF THE CROSS WE KNOW GOD IS NOT ABSENT FROM OUR SUFFERING AND PAIN.

I have an agnostic friend who cannot come to grips with the suffering he has witnessed in this world. "What can you say about a God who would allow such pain?" he asks.

Christianity does not answer the question, *Why?* God provides no answer to the intellectual dilemma—but He does give the resolution to the problem. Christ-followers look to the cross. There, in the midst of Jesus' own grief and sorrow, we see God *with us* and believe that He is able somehow to take our burdens upon Himself and deliver us from our despair. He is not distant from our pain. He understands our suffering because Jesus Christ—God in human flesh—suffered.

The cry of little Moshe was once the cry of Jesus. "Abba! Abba!" he cried in the garden of Gethsemane. "If it be possible, let this cup pass from me; nevertheless, not as I will, but as you will" (Matthew 26:39).

It is because of the cross that we know God is not absent from our suffering and pain. Because of the cross, we can experience forgiveness and reconciliation and peace with God. As we witness the evil and pain in this world, we too cry out, "*Abba! Abba!*" God does not give us an explanation. He gives us Himself. The cross is God's answer to our cry.

God Instead of Us

The cross offers a glimpse into the heart of a God who is willing to be *with* us in death and suffering. But we need more than a God who knows our pain. We need mercy for our own contributions to the pain in the world. Christ's death is not merely a picture of God *with us*. It is also a picture of a God willing to stand in our place.

Jesus Christ dies *instead of* us. He not only identifies with our suffering caused by our sin; He also enters into our sorrow and makes it His own. He takes our sin and its consequences upon Himself so that we can be free. He experiences the full force of God's wrath toward sin in order that we might be saved. Only the cross satisfies God's demand for justice and our desire for mercy.

Picture the first humans in the garden of Eden in uninterrupted fellowship with God and each other. They are called to do the will of God, but they disobey. *Not your will, Lord, but mine!* decides Adam, lurching forward to take the fruit. Thousands of years later, another garden is before us—Gethsemane. The Second Adam agonizes over the will of God, shrinking back from the cup of God's wrath, the cup He must drink for His sinful people to be spared. *Not my will, Lord, but yours!* He decides.

The essence of Adam's sin was that he put himself in God's place. The essence of Christ's obedience is that He put Himself in our place. Because of His *life* in our place, and His *death* in our stead, we are freed from our sins.

When the Romans crucified criminals in the first century, it was customary for them to nail an accusation list to the cross. The list informed people why this person was being crucified. When Jesus died, God took the accusations that Satan brings against us—all our failures and mistakes, our willful rebellion, and our constant inability to keep God's law—and God nailed those accusations to the cross of His Son. So Jesus Christ died there on Calvary, bearing your sin and mine; the accusations that should be hurled against us were hurled against Him instead.

On the cross, God demonstrated His perfect justice and His great mercy. He executed justice by pouring out His wrath against sin upon His only Son. He showed mercy by absorbing that wrath Himself, thus allowing us to escape His judgment.

Because Jesus was filled with horror and cried out, "My God, my God, why have you forsaken me?" we are filled with wonder and cry, "My God, my God, why have you *accepted* me?"

> ON THE CROSS, GOD DEMONSTRATED HIS PERFECT JUSTICE AND HIS GREAT MERCY.

Because Jesus cried, "Father, forgive!" the taunts we hurled at Him on the cross are transformed into praise for His generous mercy.

Because Jesus said, "I thirst," we can drink from the fountain of living water and never thirst again.

Because Jesus said, "Woman, behold your son," and felt the pain of separation from His earthly family, we can experience the blessing of being united with a heavenly family.

Because Jesus cried, "It is finished!" our new life can begin.

Because Jesus committed His spirit into the Father's hands, God commits His Spirit into our hearts.

Jesus is the Passover Lamb—the substitute that protects us from the wrath of God. He experienced the curse of God, the punishment for sin, the hellish torments of eternal damnation—all for the glory of God and the salvation of His people.

God for us

Anyone near the cross of Jesus on that fateful day in the first century would have thought that he was just another would-be Messiah. A miserable failure. Another leader who got caught in the crosshairs of Roman imperialism.

Satan saw this Jesus on the cross and believed he had triumphed. Jesus looked shameful. There He was—naked and bleeding, shamed and scorned and mocked. As He died, everyone thought He had been defeated.

But the truth is . . . *Satan* was being defeated. Yes, Jesus had been stripped and appeared to be defeated. Yet through His obedient death on the cross, Satan and all the forces of hell were being conquered. Satan was contributing to his own demise. Evil committed suicide when it put Jesus on the cross. As John Stott writes:

> What looks like (and indeed was) the defeat of Goodness by evil is also, and more certainly, the defeat of evil by Goodness. Overcome there, he was himself overcoming. Crushed by the ruthless power of Rome, he was himself crushing the serpent's head. The victim was the victor, and the cross is still the throne from which he rules the world.[8]

So here is the paradox: In the midst of human suffering and shame, in the midst of Christ's agony, we see the strange but wonderful plan of God—that *through this* the world would be changed. That *through this* the world would be put back together again. That through this apparent defeat, God would achieve His greatest victory. The serpent's head was crushed by the Savior's heel.

The Resurrection of Jesus

I've heard "gospel preaching" and "gospel presentations" that never got around to announcing the resurrection of Jesus Christ. Evangelicals know the cross is important, but we often imply and assume the resurrection, scratching our heads wondering why it is so important.

Every Easter pastors struggle with how to preach on the resurrection. Vague notions of "rising again to a new life" or "embracing your second chance" reflect a spiritualization of the Easter message.

It's not just pastors. C. S. Lewis' book *Mere Christianity*, a Christian classic if ever there was one, makes no mention of the resurrection. Neither does Rick Warren's book *The Purpose Driven Life*. Near the beginning, when Rick encourages people to put their faith in Christ's atoning sacrifice, he makes no mention of the empty tomb. To be fair, Warren believes in the resurrection robustly, as did Lewis. Their neglect of Easter morning is a common evangelical occurrence.

The Bible holds together the rugged cross and the empty tomb. The resurrection is important because Christ's death is important, and Christ's death is important because of His resurrection. To leave out one side of this equation is to truncate the gospel. N. T. Wright emphasizes the importance of Easter morning: "The resurrection of Jesus of Nazareth is the heart of the gospel (not to the exclusion of the cross, of course, but not least as the event which gives the cross its meaning). It is the object of faith, the ground of justification, the basis for obedient Christian living, the motivation for unity, and not least, the challenge to the principalities and powers."[9]

Vindication of Christ's Sacrifice

Here's what Christ's resurrection has accomplished. First, the resurrection of Christ proves that God has justified Jesus. In other words, in order to show the world that Jesus was innocent and that He faithfully fulfilled the vocation as God's Messiah-King, God vindicated Jesus by raising Him to new life. The resurrection is God's way of saying that Christ's sacrifice "was good." The payment for our sin was made in full. Adrian Warnock puts it this way:

> The credit of Jesus' righteousness is much larger than the debt of our sin. His account had more positive approval than the negative disapproval that was due to all of us. The debt was paid, and as a result, as a righteous man and the beloved Son of God, the Father was entirely just to raise Him. Jesus had turned away God's wrath, He had destroyed sin, our guilt could now be taken away, and we could be counted righteous. If the cross was Jesus' payment for our sins, then the resurrection marked God's acceptance of that payment.[10]

Launching a New Creation

The Gospel writers clue us in to the fact that on Easter morning, God's new world of the future (the restored universe that He has promised us) crashed into the present. Jesus didn't rise again only to die later (like Lazarus and others whom Jesus raised). He rose again to a new kind of bodily life altogether, a kind of life that was similar to our current existence and yet different in mysterious ways. As N. T. Wright explains, "The resurrection of Jesus . . . is not an absurd event within the old world but the symbol and starting point of the new world. The claim advanced in Christianity is of that magnitude: Jesus of Nazareth ushers in not simply a new religious possibility, not simply a new ethic or a new way of salvation, but a new creation."[11]

Jewish people expected that all believers would be raised on the Last Day. But Christ is the firstfruits of the future resurrection. His resurrection is the beginning of God's new world, even as the old world continues and is passing away.

The beginning of the Bible describes the garden of Eden as the place where God breathed life into Adam and gave Him the tasks of ruling and reigning. Remember where Jesus rose again? A tomb within a garden. I love the way that G.K. Chesterton describes it.

> On the third day the friends of Christ coming at daybreak to the place found the grave empty and the stone rolled away. In varying ways they realized the new wonder; but they hardly realized that the world had died in the night. What they were looking at was the first day of a new creation, with a new heaven and a new earth; and in a semblance of the gardener God walked again in the garden, in the cool not of the evening but the dawn.[12]

Defeating Death

The Eastern Orthodox Easter hymn speaks of Christ's conquering of the grave: "Christ is risen from the dead, trampling down death by death, and to those in the tombs bestowing life!" Christ's resurrection is the defeat of our great enemy: death. Sin's consequence is death; Christ's righteousness brings new life.

The New Testament scholar, George Eldon Ladd, once wrote about our need for the good news that conquers death:

> How men need this gospel! Everywhere one goes he finds the gaping graves swallowing up the dying. Tears of loss, of separation, of final departure stain every face. Every table sooner or later has an empty chair, every fireside its vacant place. Death is the great leveler. Wealth or poverty, fame or oblivion, power or futility, success or failure, race, creed or culture—all our human distinctions mean nothing before the ultimate irresistible sweep of the scythe of death which cuts us all down. And whether the mausoleum is a fabulous Taj Mahal, a massive pyramid, an unmarked spot of ragged grass or the unplotted depths of the sea

one fact stands: death reigns.

Apart from the gospel of the kingdom, death is the mighty conqueror before whom we are all helpless. . . . But the good news is this: death has been defeated; our conqueror has been conquered. In the face of the power of the kingdom of God in Christ, death was helpless. It could not hold Him, death has been defeated; life and immortality have been brought to life. An empty tomb in Jerusalem is proof of it. This is the gospel of the kingdom.[13]

The Exaltation of Jesus

One more aspect of the gospel announcement deserves to be mentioned: Jesus Christ is Lord. While it is not right to say that the gospel is *only* Jesus' lordship, neither is it biblical to exclude Jesus' lordship from the picture. Christ has been exalted as King of the world. As Peter preached so powerfully on Pentecost, "This Jesus, whom you crucified, God has made both Lord and Christ!" (Acts 2:36 NIV).

THE GOSPEL ANNOUNCEMENT: CHRIST DIED FOR OUR SINS. . . WAS RAISED ON THE THIRD DAY, AND IS NOW LORD OF THE WORLD.

Exalting Jesus in this manner caused controversy for the early Christians. On the one hand, claiming that Jesus was Lord offended many Jews. Christians were speaking of Jesus with the exalted titles reserved only for God. The early Christians were thrown out of synagogues for claiming that Jesus was not merely a prophet or a Messiah; He was God in human flesh.

On the other hand, claiming that Jesus was Lord offended many Romans. After all, Caesar was Lord. Applying Caesar's slogans and titles to Jesus implied that Christians had a greater allegiance to Jesus than to Caesar. The "gospel of Caesar" was about His ascension to the throne. Christians upstaged Caesar with the "gospel of Jesus," the crucified and risen Savior who was the true

Lord of the world.[14]

Martin Luther got it right when he summarized the basic gospel message this way: "The gospel is a story about Christ, God's and David's son, who died and was raised, and is established as Lord. This is the gospel in a nutshell."[15] This is the gospel announcement. Christ died for our sins according to the Scriptures, was raised on the third day, and is now Lord of the world.

Our Twofold Response

News this great demands a response. When the tornado siren goes off and you know the basement is safe, you can either act as if there is no danger or run quickly to safety. When my wife and I knew that our baby was about to be born, we had the choice of hurrying to the hospital or waiting around and ignoring the signs. Announcements demand responses. If the gospel announcement of Christ's death and resurrection is true, it changes everything.

The Bible gives us two words that sum up our response to the gospel announcement of Jesus Christ: *repentance* and *faith*.

Repentance

Repentance is a churchy word that often gets reduced to a simple display of emotion. We tend to think of repentance as feeling sorry for our sin. Of course, feeling sorry is a part of repentance, but it is not all that biblical repentance entails. When my son gets caught doing something wrong, he feels sorry. But there's a difference between being sorry because you have to face consequences and being sorry for having sinned.

True repentance is not merely an expression of sadness over the damage our sin has caused to ourselves, to our family and friends, and to our world. True repentance begins with a vertical dimension. We are sorry for how our sin has attacked the heart of God. We have violated God's law. We have put ourselves in His place. True repentance sees sin for what it is. As we agree with God about our sin and ask Him for forgiveness, we turn away from sin and move in the opposite direction. We don't just regret our sins and the harm that they cause. We fight sin. We seek to live according to the Scriptures.

Our expression of repentance is immediate and lifelong. Our initial repentance before God leads us to seek forgiveness from the people we sin against. This is the horizontal dimension.

This turn from sin is sudden, yet it continues in the life of a Christian until we are made new in God's kingdom and we are saved to sin no more. The difference between Christians and unbelievers today is not that Christians are perfect while unbelievers still sin. The difference is that Christians mourn over their sin, find forgiveness in Christ, and then fight sin through the power of the Holy Spirit. We give up our own personal agendas and choose to seek first God's kingdom.

Faith

A number of pop songs extol the virtue of "faith." Singers, movie stars, and TV celebrities all praise the idea of believing in something, whether it's God, a higher power, or yourself. But much of this talk about "faith" is simply belief *in belief*. It is devoid of any objective content.

How does this work out practically? People start to think that it doesn't really matter *what* you believe about God, so long as you believe. What's important is faith, not theology. The key is *that* you believe, not *what* you believe.

But what happens if whatever you believe in lets you down? What happens if the object of your faith isn't worthy of your faith?

Picture yourself in an airplane with an inexperienced pilot. Once you are in the air, the plane begins to malfunction. As the plane nose-dives, you continue to trust in that pilot. You close

TRUE FAITH HAS POWER BECAUSE OF WHO WE BELIEVE IN.

your eyes and think, *It's important that I have faith. I believe! I believe!* Unfortunately, no matter how much faith you place in that pilot, if he is unworthy of your trust, your plane will still crash. Faith or no faith—it's the pilot that matters!

In the same way, Christian faith is not generic. It's not just important that you believe something, but that the Someone you believe in is actually able to save you! True faith has power because of *who we believe in,* not simply *because we believe.*

I'm not saying that all that matters is that a person nods his or her head and affirms a few biblical doctrines about God. Even demons have that kind of faith. The truth is, faith includes sincerity *and* genuine commitment. Saving faith includes the objective content of the Christian gospel (the life, death, and resurrection of Jesus Christ) *and* the subjective feelings that indicate true heart transformation (trust and sincerity). Take one without the other and you have a counterfeit.

News That Changed the World

When we hear the good news of Jesus' death and resurrection, the Holy Spirit stirs up repentance in our hearts and grants us faith. We come to the end of ourselves and realize that we have nothing to contribute to our salvation. So we place our faith in Christ alone. We call this doctrine "justification by faith." God justifies us or declares us righteous. He does so not because of anything we have done, but because we are united to Jesus Christ, who has this righteous standing before God in our place.

Pronouncements change things:

"You're fired!"

"I now pronounce you husband and wife."

"And the winner is . . . "

"It's a boy!"

The gospel announcement of Jesus Christ is just as powerful. This news has changed the world, and as we proclaim this announcement, we find that it changes people too.

Scripture Truths

ON THE NEW BIRTH: *John 3:1–21; 16:16–24; 1 Peter 1:3–25*

ON THE GOSPEL ANNOUNCEMENT: *Isaiah 52:7; Mark 1:14–15; 1 Corinthians 15:1–6; Romans 1:1–4; 2 Timothy 2:8*

ON BEING A WITNESS TO THE POWER OF THE GOSPEL: *John 4:1–42; 9; Acts 22:1–21; 26*

ON JESUS' DEMONSTRATIONS OF THE ARRIVAL OF THE KINGDOM: *Mark 1:14–15, 29–34; 4:35–41; 6:30–44; John 11:1–44*

ON THE RIGHTEOUSNESS OF CHRIST: *Romans 5:12–21; 2 Corinthians 5:16–21*

ON THE ATONEMENT: *Romans 3:25; 2 Corinthians 5:19; Galatians 1:4; 3:13; Ephesians 2:13; Colossians 2:14–15; Hebrews 2:14–18; 1 Peter 2:24; 3:18; 1 John 3:8; 4:10*

ON THE CENTRALITY OF THE RESURRECTION: *Psalm 49:7–15; Matthew 28; Mark 16; Luke 24; John 20–21; Acts 17:18; Romans 4:24–25; 10:9; 1 Corinthians 15; 1 Peter 1:3; 3:21*

ON THE EXALTATION OF JESUS: *Acts 1; 2:14–41; Romans 10:9; Philippians 2:1–11; Colossians 1:15–23; 1 Timothy 3:16*

ON REPENTANCE AND FAITH: *Matthew 3:2; Mark 1:15; Luke 5:32; John 3:16–18; 6:35; 7:38; 14:1; Acts 2:38; 16:31; 20:17–21; 26:19–23; Romans 1:16; 5:1; 2 Corinthians 7:10; Ephesians 1:13; 2 Peter 3:9*

The cruelty in reducing the gospel to nagging is the despair it produces.

– C. FitzSimons Allison

the moralistic gospel

I HAVE A friend who recently moved from the "buckle" of the Bible Belt to the beautiful state of Utah. In a large town not far from Salt Lake City, my friend has answered God's call to preach the gospel and serve Christ's church in one of the most pristine places in the United States. Though the rest of the country is in a recession, this area boasts a booming economy. People are generally pleasant and honest. Children are polite. There is very little alcoholism. It's a big city, but the crime rate is astoundingly low.

Here the majority of the population attends worship services every week, so most businesses are closed on Sundays. Anyone hoping for a family-friendly environment would love to live here.

Yet this place is one of the darkest in America. In the Mormon temples that dot the landscape, the true Christ is not preached. The culture is grounded in traditional morality, but Christ is missing. My friend has the difficult task of preaching the gospel —not to those who recognize their desperate need for a Savior, but to a population who sees moral, upright behavior as the goal of all their religious fervor.

Evangelical Versions of Moralism

When I was a kid, I enjoyed looking through coloring books for the "What's missing?" page. The point of the exercise is to discover that something integral to the picture *isn't there*. It's fun to scan the details of the page looking for an omission so obvious you may overlook its absence!

I wonder if our churches sometimes resemble the "What's missing?" page in coloring books. We have the trappings of religion around us. We are grounded in traditional morality, and we say we are all about life change. We look down our noses on cults like the Mormons and Jehovah's Witnesses for missing the biblical Christ. But could it be that much of our own talk about God is spiritually vague? Perhaps the question is not so much "What's missing?" in our churches but "Who's missing?" Do we focus on Christ and what He has done? The ever-present danger for the church is the same for each of our hearts—to turn from the gospel to *moralism*.

What is moralism and how does it play out in our lives? Here are a few ways to spot it:

Getting Right with God without Defining Who God Is

Ever since I was a kid I've been attending "revival services" in the church. The idea is to invite a traveling evangelist for a week-long marathon of good preaching. Patterned after Billy Graham's crusades, these services are evangelistically oriented. Church members are urged to invite unsaved friends and neighbors to hear the gospel.

I can recall some revival services where the gospel announcement has been clearly proclaimed by an evangelist pleading for people to throw themselves upon the mercy of Christ. Other times, speakers have urged people to "get right with God," but they never clearly explained who Jesus is and what He has done.

I once assisted at a Vacation Bible School in which a special speaker came on the last night to wrap up the week with a gospel presentation. The message went something like this: "We've all made mistakes. But if you believe that Jesus wants to forgive you, you can be saved." There was no cross. No resurrection. No mention of what we would need to be saved from.

I was left wondering, *Is there anything in that "gospel presentation" that a Mormon wouldn't affirm?* Thankfully, several of the counselors recognized the deficiency and filled in the gaps for the children afterwards.

Let me be clear. I believe that we need to call for people to trust in Christ. Urgently calling people to repentance and faith is essential. But in calling for decisions, let us not forget to tell people *why* they should come to Christ! Otherwise, we fail to clearly describe the God we come to know in Jesus. We fail to teach them that the God who justifies us is the same God who sanctifies us. In the end, we leave people with the idea that God will wipe their slate clean but that it's up to them to turn around and change their lives.

Proclaiming Good Advice Instead of Good News

Another way that we slowly move away from the gospel and toward a moralistic counterfeit is in thinking that Christianity is basically about being a good person. The emphasis always should be on what God has done for us in Christ. Yet sometimes we replace this with an emphasis on rules and other things Christians should do to be "good Christians." When morality becomes the essence of Christianity, we change the good news into good advice. Giving people good advice about how to live is easy to do. Not only that, it's popular with the audience.

Still, if we're not careful, we may cause people to think that

Christianity is all about our goodness and the good works that we are to do, not about the goodness of Christ demonstrated in what He has already done. We temper the explosive news of a crucified and risen King Jesus with the more palatable message that our life can improve if we simply make a place for God. The message may center on improving your family life, getting control over your finances, or having a better marriage. Or maybe the gospel becomes advice on how to improve your self-esteem, how to live longer, or how to feel good by taking care of others.

Good advice sells books, but the gospel changes hearts. Good advice is popular, but the gospel is *powerful.*

Beginning with Grace, Then Turning Back to Law

Not too long ago, I purchased a new computer with a new operating system. Microsoft promised a smooth experience, but the updates drove me nuts. Whenever I turned on the computer in the morning, I'd suffer a slow wait as my hard drive "cooked" in the background. Updates loading . . . reinstallations . . . time to reboot. The updates were supposed to increase the health of my computer, but instead they became a source of constant frustration.

Sometimes we face the same trouble in our walk with Christ. When we first come to faith, we are overwhelmed by the grace of God proclaimed to us in the gospel. The gospel is our new operating system, and a life of spiritual productivity follows our being justified by faith.

Over time, however, we revert back to a law-centered life. Perhaps it's what we hear in church, from other Christians, or in pop evangelicalism. The law comes back like the updates on my computer. We may have started with the gospel as our operating system, but we think we need law updates in order to make life smoother.

Unfortunately, spiritual productivity slows and frustration builds. Going back to the law bogs us down and causes us to question our devotion and assurance. Just as we want to yell at our computer and say, "What's wrong with you?" when it's moving at a snail's pace, we pull our hair out when we see our lack of spiritual progress and say, "Something must be wrong with me!"

Slowly but surely, the gospel that we began with—that glorious truth that Christ loved us and gave Himself for us—is bogged down in updates that aren't grounded in that message. So we think, *Yes, the gospel is the operating system, but now the updates are where it's at.*

The law is a good gift from God that shows us the heart of God and reveals our need for salvation. But the law is not a daily supplement to grace.

Too many times we think, *Of course, we are saved by grace, but . . .* That "but" is deadly. It indicates that we think something other than grace will bring life transformation. It doesn't matter what good activity you put after that "but" (*now you need to tithe, now you need to give up this or that, now you need to evangelize*). The "but" bogs the operating system down in updates.

Life transformation doesn't follow "but"; it follows "so now." *You are saved by grace,* so now *you are free to live for God in this way or that.* Life change is grounded in the gospel alone, not in the law's updates.

The Christian life will never run the way it is supposed to if law is the fuel. The gospel alone has to be the engine. All our good works must flow from sheer gratitude, not an updates-based system that keeps telling me to reboot and start again.

Spiritualizing the Gospel Announcement

Another way that we can turn from the gospel to moralism is to spiritualize the good news. Instead of focusing on the history of Christ's life, death, and resurrection, we can use the Christian story thematically in order to provide a message of self-help.

For example, we turn the message of Christ's resurrection into something like this: "Christ has been raised! So now you need to realize you have the power to get up too. Here's your chance to make a new start." See what we've done? We've taken the mind-blowing, world-altering message of a dead man walking out of the grave and turned it into a spiritualized version of self-help teaching that you can find anywhere else.

We all tend to move in this direction. Any of us can slide quickly into spiritualization if we're not careful. Mark Galli tells a funny story about being challenged in this area:

> A group of Laotian refugees who had been attending the Sacramento church I pastored approached me after the service one Sunday and asked to become members. Our church had sponsored them, and they had been attending the church only a few months. They had only a rudimentary understanding of the Christian faith, so I suggested we study the Gospel of Mark together for a few weeks, to make sure they knew what a commitment to Christ and His church entailed. They happily agreed.
>
> Despite the Laotians' lack of Christian knowledge—or maybe because of it—the Bible studies were some of the most interesting I've ever led. After we read the passage in which Jesus calms the storm, I began as I usually did with more theologically sophisticated groups: I asked them about the storms in their lives. There was a puzzled look among my Laotian friends, so I elaborated: we all have storms—problems, worries, troubles, crises—and this story teaches that Jesus can give us peace in the midst of those storms. "So what are your storms?" I asked.
>
> Again, more puzzled silence. Finally, one of the men hesitantly asked, "Do you mean Jesus actually calmed the wind and sea in the middle of a storm?"
>
> I thought he was finding the story incredulous, and I didn't want to get distracted with the problem of miracles. So I replied, "Yes, but we should not get hung up on the details of the miracle.

We should remember that Jesus can calm the storms in our lives."

Another stretch of awkward silence ensued until another replied, "Well, if Jesus calmed the wind and the waves, he must be a very powerful man!" At this, they all nodded vigorously and chattered excitedly to one another in Lao. Except for me, the room was full of awe and wonder.

I suddenly realized that they grasped the story better than I did, and I finally acknowledged, "Yes, Jesus is a very powerful person. In fact, Christians believe he is the Creator of heaven and earth, and thus, of course, he has power over the wind and the waves."[1]

Galli's personal anecdote demonstrates what we lose whenever we substitute the explosiveness of the gospel announcement for a spiritualized version of self-help: awe and wonder. We lose our sense of awe at the God who has acted so powerfully in human history, and then we lose our sense of wonder at God's grace.

SPOTTING THE COUNTERFEIT

the moralistic gospel

STORY	ANNOUNCEMENT	COMMUNITY
Our sinful condition is seen as the individual sins we commit. Redemption comes through the exercise of willpower with God's help.	The good news is spiritual instruction about what we can do to win God's favor and blessing upon our earthly endeavors.	The church is a place where people who believe like us can affirm each other in keeping the standards of the community.

Why This Counterfeit Is Attractive

Like all of the counterfeits in this book, the moralistic gospel has a certain appeal. Here are some of the reasons we find this gospel so attractive:

The moralistic gospel is safe.

Moralism primarily attacks the gospel announcement by changing the news about Jesus into a new motivation for changing your own life. This alteration leads to a twisted view of the fall, as our problem becomes our sins (plural) more than our sin (singular). The Bible teaches that sin is a condition we are born with. Our sinful actions come from a wicked heart. The moralistic gospel casts us as good people battling "sins."

Why is this counterfeit safe? Because you can devise sin lists that are easy to manage. *You* stay in control. Just figure out which sins you want to get control of and then work on fighting them. Simple as that!

The Christian life is turned into three or four easy steps. You gain the approval from God that you need by modifying your behavior. Even if you don't think that you are sinless, you are at least *trying*. That's what counts. Righteousness comes by trying to meet whatever moral expectations you or your church has set up for you. God no longer expects perfection, merely improvement. So the church comes along like Home Depot and says, "You can do it. We can help!"

The moralistic gospel appeals to our longing for universal morality.

Not too long ago, I had lunch with a college student who was wrestling with some of the moral teaching he had grown up with. He had made some new friends who didn't hold the same moral standards that he had learned in church. As we talked, it became clear that he saw his parents and church as being unnecessarily judgmental. "Who's to say that certain behaviors are wrong? That's not any of our business."

As I pressed him about some of his new acquaintances, I pointed out that his new friends were just as judgmental as the strict conservative folks he knew in church. His friends cast judgment on people who didn't recycle or eat organic foods. They had merely exchanged moral standards.

In *Policy Review*, Mary Eberstadt compares two imaginary ladies, a grandmother named Betty and her thirty-year-old granddaughter, Jennifer. Betty wouldn't think of judging someone based upon what they eat. Jennifer wouldn't think of judging someone based upon their sexual activity. But both still maintain some notion that there is right and wrong.

> [W]hat the imaginary examples of Betty and [her thirty-year-old granddaughter] Jennifer have established is this: Their personal moral relationships toward food and toward sex are just about perfectly reversed. Betty does care about nutrition and food, but it doesn't occur to her to extend her opinions to a moral judgment—i.e., to believe that other people ought to do as she does in the matter of food, and that they are wrong if they don't. In fact, she thinks such an extension would be wrong in a different way; it would be impolite, needlessly judgmental, simply not done. Jennifer, similarly, does care to some limited degree about what other people do about sex; but it seldom occurs to her to extend her opinions to a moral judgment. In fact, she thinks such an extension would be wrong in a different way—because it would be impolite, needlessly judgmental, simply not done.
>
> On the other hand, Jennifer is genuinely certain that her opinions about food are not only nutritionally correct, but also, in some deep, meaningful sense, morally correct—i.e., she feels that others ought to do something like what she does. And Betty, on the other hand, feels exactly the same way about what she calls sexual morality.[2]

Do you see how the desire to judge is woven into the core of our being? Generations may trade morals and values, but all of us long for universal morality. We are born to be moralists. God has given us a conscience that reveals to us that something is wrong with the world. Likewise, deep down we know that something is wrong *with us*.

Moralism satisfies our desire for a universal morality in a perverse way. We look for ways to define our morality based upon whatever is socially acceptable. By shifting with the moral standards of society, we feel good about staying within current expressions of morality and rejecting older expressions of morality. Ironically, what may look like license is actually a commitment to new moral norms.

DEEP DOWN WE KNOW THAT SOMETHING IS WRONG *WITH US*.

Unfortunately, adapting to the changing morals of society will never change our hearts. We settle for looking good on the outside by upholding certain moral conventions. The moralistic gospel appeals to our desire for morality and goodness. But moralism can make us into nice upstanding citizens and still lead straight to hell.

The moralistic gospel emphasizes transformed character.
One other reason that this counterfeit is attractive is because it rightly understands that salvation should result in the transformation of our character. Too many Christians profess Christ with their lips but deny Him by the way that they live.

The problem? *Christians aren't behaving!* The solution? *Let's teach them how to behave.* So we drill the law into new converts as the way to get people to start acting like Christians. We make the gospel merely the entry point into the Christian family and behavioral modification the bread and butter of Christian living.

Unfortunately, in making behavioral change the focus rather

than the result of the gospel, we assert control over our relationship with God. We assume that the gospel is to justify and that the law is to make us holy, when actually the gospel is the fuel that empowers all of the Christian life. Good works are always the fruit, never the root, of gospel change.

Countering the Counterfeit

So how do we counter a moralistic gospel that reduces the good news to behavioral improvement? How can we avoid embracing the counterfeit? The only solution is to see the moralistic gospel as a shrunken and shriveled version of the glorious gospel of grace. It is to the biblical gospel that we must now turn.

Recognize that true transformation comes from the biblical gospel.

Not long ago, I received an e-mail from a college student whom I regularly pray for. This young man is seeking to be faithful to Christ. After going through a difficult time of trying to obtain victory over certain sins, he said, "I think my foundation had shifted from the gospel to self-righteousness. I think I had felt I mortified my sins, but in reality I taught them to sit, stay, and play dead. Training sin is much like trying to train [a wild] animal. You can teach a bear tricks, but eventually it will attack. Subtle sins attacked me. I was at a point in my life where I felt I couldn't even pray. I would try, and it was futile. I came face to face with men's curse of being subjected to futility."

I can relate to this e-mail. My heart is constantly sliding back to a moralistic framework of understanding the gospel. The moralistic gospel says, "Do better!" When we don't do better, the counterfeit tries to fix us by giving us even *more* commands.

But the message that continually says, "Shape up!" isn't what leads to lasting change. Though it might offer us temporary improvements, the counterfeit is powerless to effect true transformation. Only the gospel can change us, because only the gospel gives us grace. The moralistic gospel twists the notion of grace into something that is deserved, as if God would say, "I will show grace to you *because you deserve it.*" But that's not grace at all. God's grace is demonstrated in that while we were still sinners, Christ died for us!

WE WANT TO PROVE TO GOD . . . THAT WE ARE SOMEHOW GOOD ENOUGH.

The gospel operates from a completely different principle than moralistic religion. As Tim Keller writes, "Religion operates on the principle 'I obey—therefore I am accepted by God.' But the operating principle of the gospel is 'I am accepted by God through what Christ has done—therefore I obey.'"[3]

The moralistic gospel is the default setting of the human heart. We are constantly drifting toward self-justification. We want to prove to God and to ourselves that we are somehow good enough.

We see a perfect picture of the moralistic understanding at work in the parable of the prodigal son. We're all familiar with the younger brother in the story. He rebels by heading to the far country and wasting all of his money in extravagant living, in clear rebellion against his father. But the older brother in the story is just as rebellious, even if he is the dutiful son who stays at home. He may be close to the father, but his heart is far away. Thus when the prodigal returns and the father slaughters the fatted calf, the older brother complains.

There are two ways to run from God. One way is to rebel against Him publicly by breaking all the rules. The other way is to rebel against Him inwardly by trying to keep all the rules and therefore establish yourself as your own personal savior. As Keller writes, "Ironically, you may be looking to Jesus as a teacher, model, and helper, but you are avoiding Him as savior. You are trusting in your own goodness rather than in Jesus for your standing with God. You are trying to save yourself by following Jesus."[4]

This counterfeit exists in every culture I've ministered in. During my first year in Romania, I had a conversation with a young man who had been frequenting our church. His biggest hang-up with putting his trust in Christ was that he didn't think he could master his sins. There were certain sins that he felt he could conquer, but there were a few that he wasn't sure he could let go.

I told him, "I don't think you can give up those sins either." He was shocked by my response.

"You don't think I can change?" he said, completely thrown off by my statement.

"No, I don't," I told him. "And you will *never* change as long as you think you have to change before trusting in Christ."

I explained again the nature of grace—that life transformation is not the *cause* of God's grace, but the *result* of God's grace. My friend was trying to earn salvation through sheer willpower. But salvation comes not through our willpower, but through *God's* will and power.

My friend later told me that our conversation completely flipped his thinking. He had never considered grace to be completely undeserved. A few days later, he became a Christian, and those sins he was so concerned about melted away under the warmth of God's grace.

More recently, I was witnessing to someone who lived in the South. He had been attending church and was beginning to open up to the gospel. But his reasons for postponing his decision were similar to that of the Romanian teenager: *I need to get control over this sin before I come to Christ.*

It would have been unbiblical for me to deny the importance of life change. It's not enough to tell someone, "Grace accepts you as you are. Don't worry about your sin!" We must make clear that grace accepts us where we are, but that it never leaves us there. At the same time, we must make clear that the biblical gospel is transformative precisely because it is a gift from a God who is not obligated to save us. The gospel's power gripped this man too, and I had the privilege of baptizing him several weeks later.

Repent from a heart broken by sin and overwhelmed by grace. Fifty years ago, many evangelicals were caricatured with the following statement: "You don't drink or smoke or chew or go with girls who do." Worldliness was defined as a handful of habits: movies, card games, etc. Messages against these practices thundered from the pulpit.

TO AVOID THE COUNTERFEIT GOSPEL OF MORALISM [WE MUST] COME FACE TO FACE WITH THE GRAVITY OF OUR SIN.

In a moralistic world, repentance is sin-management. Salvation is about getting control of the sins on your church's sin list, so that you can then achieve respectability. We still do the same thing today, even if our list of sins has changed.

But this view of sin is woefully inadequate. King David asked God to expose even his hidden faults. He knew that he was sinful to the core. He didn't want to merely stop committing a few sins. He needed transformation of the heart, which would then lead to behavioral change. Charles Spurgeon once said that repenting of the evil act and not the evil heart is like men pumping water out of a leaking ship but forgetting to stop the leak!

The only way to avoid the counterfeit gospel of moralism is to come face to face with the gravity of our sin. Once we see our desperate situation, we must turn to Christ for deliverance. The moralistic gospel would have us turn to Christ for help. The biblical gospel points to Christ for rescue.

Repentance comes from a God-given sense of brokenness over our sin. We stop comparing ourselves to the people around us and start comparing ourselves to God. Once we see ourselves in light of God's holiness, and once we see the magnificent grace that has come to us *despite our sin,* we recognize that we do not stand before God as "better sinners" or "worse sinners." We are either unrepentant or repentant. True Christianity hinges on repentance—being broken over our sin and being gripped by the marvelous grace of a God who has chosen to save us.

Give up your rights and rest in God's finished work.

How do you know if you have fallen for the moralistic counterfeit? Here are two easy diagnostics:

First, think about how you react to suffering and pain. How do you view God when you pass through a terrible trial? Moralists immediately think, *What have I done to deserve this? Doesn't God see all the good I've done?* Because you see God as a sort of cosmic employer, you have certain expectations of Him. When God doesn't meet these expectations, you become angry. Eventually, your disillusionment leads to despair. You think that all your efforts at pleasing God must be useless.

The second diagnostic is to check your heart whenever you see someone else benefiting from God's grace. Not too long ago, I found out that an acquaintance had recently been given a new ministry opportunity and a promotion. How did my heart respond to this news? By sinking into jealousy rather than leaping for joy. The thoughts that raced through my mind (*Why did God do that for* him *and not me? Am I not deserving?*) stood in opposition to grace. I had to repent again and ask God to so change my heart that I would rejoice in His grace being showered on others.

The moralistic gospel resembles the famous Bob Newhart skit, in which his counsel to broken people seeking change is to continually yell, "Stop it!" To be sure, the New Testament contains many commands. But notice that God's commands are always grounded in God's past actions. The imperatives (commands) are based in indicatives—statements about what God has done.

Tullian Tchividjian puts it this way: "Imperatives divorced from indicatives become impossibilities."[5] This is the logic of the gospel. You can see the journey from indicative to imperative running throughout Paul's letters, most often turning on the word "therefore."

"You are not under law but under grace" and you "have been brought from death to life" (*indicatives* Romans 6:14, 13), *therefore*, "let not sin therefore reign in your mortal body. . . . Do not present your members to sin as instruments for unrighteousness, but present yourselves to God as those who have been brought from death to life, and your members to God as instruments for righteousness" (*imperatives* Romans 6: 12–13).

The first three chapters of Ephesians explain the gospel in terms of God's redemptive plan, our powerlessness to save ourselves, and God's bringing together Jew and Gentile alike. Then in chapter 4, Paul begins to list ways to apply the gospel message. "Therefore," he says and proceeds to give us commands that are grounded in the gospel.

Or take a look at Galatians 5:24 and 16: "Those who belong to Christ Jesus have crucified the flesh with its passions and desires" [*indicative*], *therefore*, "walk by the Spirit, and you will not gratify the desires of the flesh" [*imperative*].

If we focus our attention on what *we* are to do without grounding our lives in what Christ has *done*, we will become disillusioned. That's why so many people who never seem to get any traction in the Christian life walk the aisle again and again. They recommit their lives to Christ, saying, "I'll try harder this time! I'll be more serious!" only to become deflated and disappointed that they feel no power in their Christian life.

The result of the moralistic gospel is despair. But that despair is what can and should lead us to the biblical gospel of grace— the true gospel that exposes the counterfeit and brings lasting behavioral change, precisely because it's not first about outward change but inward transformation by the cross of Jesus Christ.

Bask in the glory of God's grace.

The apostle Paul writes that we are not justified by works of the law but through faith in Christ Jesus. We are justified by faith alone, saved by grace alone because of what Christ has done on our behalf.

The moralistic gospel may fill our churches with well-behaved people. But the result will merely be an improved version of the old man—not the new man that the biblical gospel promises. Without grace, we miss out on true life transformation.

There was once a British conference on comparative religions. People from all over the world were debating the uniqueness of the Christian faith. They were discussing the ideas of resurrection, heaven, eternality of the soul, good works, and love for one's neighbor. The famous writer C. S. Lewis came into the room. Over the course of his life, he had moved from a position of atheism to agnosticism, and then to Christianity. Some of the men at the conference decided to ask Lewis what was unique about Christianity. Lewis replied, "Oh, that's easy. It's grace."[5]

Grace accomplishes what moralism promises, but can never deliver: a changed heart. One of the most powerful literary examples of grace comes from Victor Hugo's *Les Miserables*. In the story, we meet a common thief, Jean Valjean, who is befriended by an elderly and kind bishop. Valjean responds to the kindness of this bishop by stealing expensive silverware and running away. Once he is apprehended, he is dragged by the police back to the bishop. Then the bishop does the unthinkable:

> "Ah, there you are!" he cried, looking straight at Jean Valjean.
> "Am I glad to see you! But, heavens! I gave you the candlesticks
> too, you know; they are made of silver like the rest and you can

get two hundred francs for them, easily. Why didn't you take them with the cutlery?"

Jean Valjean's eyes nearly popped out of his head; he looked at the venerable bishop with an expression no human tongue could convey.

"Monseigneur," said the sergeant, "is what this man said true, then? We saw him hotfooting it out of town. He looked like he was on the run. So we arrested him to be on the safe side. He had all this silver—"

"And he told you," the bishop broke in with a smile, "that it had been given to him by some old codger of a priest whose place he'd spent the night in? I can see how it looks. So you've brought him back here? There has been a misunderstanding". . .

"My dear friend," said the bishop [to Jean Valjean], "before you go, here are your candlesticks. Take them."

He went to the mantelpiece, swept up the two candlesticks, and handed them over to Jean Valjean. . . . Jean Valjean's whole body was shaking. He took the two candlesticks automatically and with a stricken look on his face.

"Now," said the bishop, "go in peace."[7]

Jean Valjean leaves the bishop's house, stunned by the grace being shown to him:

He did not recognize himself. He could not make sense of what was happening to him. He steeled himself against the old man's angelic act and against his gentle words . . . He defended himself against such heavenly forgiveness by means of pride, which is like a stronghold of evil inside us.

Grace is offensive. It chipped away at this old thief's heart. Not long after being forgiven by the bishop, Valjean robs a young child. Now that Valjean has been the recipient of undeserved favor, his sin propels him into a moment of crisis. He sees himself for who he is in light of the grace that has been shown to him. At once, his heart and mind are forever changed, conquered by grace. Here is how Victor Hugo described the moment:

> Jean Valjean cried for a long time. He shed hot tears, he sobbed, more helpless and fragile than any woman, more terrified than any child.
>
> While he was crying, day dawned brighter and brighter in his spirit, and it was an extraordinary light, a light at once ravishing and terrible.[8]

The rest of the story describes the life of this forgiven and repentant thief, Jean Valjean. The grace of Christ shown through a bishop led to true life change. And the grace of God in our Lord Jesus Christ does the same for us as well.

Scripture Truths

ON THE TWO WAYS TO RUN FROM GOD: *Luke 15:11–32*

ON THE NEED FOR HEART TRANSFORMATION: *Psalms 19:12–14; 51; Ezekiel 11:19; 36:2–6; Romans 7:7–25*

ON SCRIPTURAL COMMANDS GROUNDED IN GOD'S WORK: *Romans 6:12–14; Galatians 5; Colossians 3*

ON JUSTIFICATION BY FAITH: *Romans 3:28; Galatians 2:16; 3:11; James 2:18–26; Titus 3:3–7; 2 Timothy 1:8–9*

I am neither an optimist nor a pessimist.
Jesus Christ is risen from the dead.

– Lesslie Newbigin

the quietist gospel

IN HIS BOOK chronicling the deception of the German people during the rise of Adolf Hitler, Erwin Lutzer relates the first-person story of a man who lived in Germany during World War II:

> I lived in Germany during the Nazi Holocaust. I considered myself a Christian. We heard stories of what was happening to the Jews, but we tried to distance ourselves from it, because, what could anyone do to stop it?
>
> A railroad track ran behind our small church and each Sunday morning we could hear the whistle in the distance and then the wheels coming over the tracks. We became disturbed when we heard the cries coming from the train as it passed by. We realized that it was carrying Jews like cattle in the cars!
>
> Week after week the whistle would blow. We dreaded to hear the sound of those wheels because we knew that we would hear the cries of the Jews en route to a death camp. Their screams tormented us.

We knew the time the train was coming and when we heard the whistle blow we began singing hymns. By the time the train came past our church we were singing at the top of our voices. If we heard the screams, we sang more loudly and soon we heard them no more.

Years have passed and no one talks about it anymore. But I still hear that train whistle in my sleep. God forgive me; forgive all of us who called ourselves Christians yet did nothing to intervene.[1]

If you are like me, this kind of story sends shivers up your spine. How could so many churches ignore the evil realities taking place all around them? How could so many professing Christians remain silent in the face of such horrific atrocities? Perhaps what happened in Germany was an aberration, we think, trying to console ourselves.

But a brief look at our own history shows Christians often complicit in some of the great evils of the day. Slavery is a sad example. I shudder when reading reports from slaves describing the treatment they received from Bible-believing, church-going Christians. One slave reported that his master served him Communion at church in the morning and whipped him in the afternoon for returning to the plantation a few minutes late.[2]

As evangelicals, we believe the gospel transforms our lives. Because of our emphasis on transformation, we can fall into one of two traps. One trap confuses the effects of the gospel with the gospel itself. Our efforts at making the world a better place can replace the verbal proclamation of the good news. (I've labeled this error "the activist gospel" and will address it in an upcoming chapter.)

Another trap is to react against the activists by retreating into a private sphere in which the light of the gospel is hidden under a bowl. Our focus becomes the church for the church, rather than the church *for the world*. I call this "the quietist gospel."

What Is the Quietist Gospel?

The biblical gospel is about events that have happened in history. Jesus Christ has died for our sins, been raised from the dead, and He is Lord. The good news is *public* news—with implications relevant for every human, every state, every nation, and every continent. In contrast, the quietist-gospel counterfeit strikes at the heart of the gospel as a public announcement and turns the good news into a message that is *only* personal. The counterfeit says that the cross and resurrection of Jesus Christ no longer address the world, but only the individual.

In the aftermath of the quietist gospel, the church loses its distinctive mission and becomes an enclave of like-minded individuals who work for their own survival. Redemption and restoration are shrunk down to an other-worldly, disembodied existence after death, rather than the promise of a new earth— a society in which righteousness dwells. The church develops a defensive posture of purity (so as to escape from the world) instead of developing a corporate holiness that is *on offense* (so as to display the glory of God in calling others to repentance).

Evangelical Versions of the Quietist Gospel

The quietist gospel is a very subtle counterfeit. Few Christian leaders would say that the gospel has no implications for public life. Yet one can glimpse quietist tendencies in a number of statements. Here are a few examples:

"The gospel is only about individual salvation."

TV commentator and author Glenn Beck recently made headlines by warning people that liberal political views were being baptized in Christian lingo. He said, in no uncertain terms, that the gospel is about individual salvation only. Of course, Beck is a Mormon and hardly an evangelical. But surprisingly, a number of evangelicals rushed to defend Beck's statement.

To be fair to Beck, this statement was uttered in a context in which, unfortunately, many preachers have abandoned or neglected the biblical gospel and promoted a political or economic cause. It is true that the gospel is not a message about social reform. Yet the gospel announcement births a community of redeemed sinners who seek to be faithful to Christ in all walks of life, and this announcement certainly has social implications. When Jesus' mother Mary sang to the Lord, rejoicing in His favor and grace shown to her personally, she also saw good news in God's promise to bring down the mighty and lift up the humble.

To neglect a message of forgiveness of sins for individuals is to tear out the heart of the gospel. But to say that the gospel announcement is *only* about individual salvation leads to a denial of the public ramifications of what we confess.

One of the Easter songs I most enjoyed growing up was the hymn "He Lives." Nowadays, I can't get past the quietist tendencies of the lyrics. The chorus declares, rightly, "Christ Jesus lives today", then adding: "He walks with me and talks with me along life's narrow way." The reason you and I can "know He lives" is because "He lives within my heart."[3]

I'm sure the writer of "He Lives" and the many evangelicals who sing this song believe in an historical, literal resurrection of Jesus' body. But you wouldn't know it from the lyrics. The chorus makes it seem like Christ's resurrection took place so that He could keep us company. The proof of the resurrection lies not within the empty tomb, but within our happy hearts. Notice how the explosive claim that Jesus of Nazareth's heart began beating again on the third day after His crucifixion is spiritualized, personalized, and privatized. I'm not accusing the writer of "He Lives" of abandoning the faith; I'm merely pointing out how easy it is for us to individualize salvation to the point that even a world-changing event like the resurrection is shrunk to a quiet message of personal peace.

"The only role that Christians have in society is evangelism."

When asked why God doesn't simply take new believers straight to heaven to be with Him, some pastors respond by saying, "We must stay on earth to tell others about Jesus." Of course, evangelism is a Christian responsibility, but it isn't right to take that statement a step further and say "The only role we have in society is evangelism." To neglect evangelism is to deny the main thrust of Christ's Great Commission. But to make evangelism the *only* responsibility of Christians in public life is to create a two-tiered hierarchy of Christians.

Think about it. Most Christians are ordinary people who work week to week in all sorts of vocations. We wake up in the morning, go to work, spend most of our time fulfilling our duty as an employee, and then rest a little in the evening before going to bed. Even if we spend time in the morning in prayer and Bible study, that time is small compared to all the other responsibilities we must fulfill. One of our Christian tasks is to testify to the gospel, especially with the people we work with. But the majority of our time is spent seeking to do our jobs well to the glory of God.

If we elevate evangelism to the point that everything else we do is considered unimportant or merely temporal, we weigh down fellow Christians with guilt they shouldn't have to carry. We lift up the super-Christians who are involved in church ministry, whether as pastors or evangelists or missionaries. We act as if *they* are the ones who are *truly* fulfilling the Great Commission. Everyone else is ordinary and perhaps too devoted to temporal things.

This dichotomy is unhealthy. When we forget that *all* we do should be to the glory of God and for the good of our neighbor, we divide our activities into categories of "sacred" and "secular." And Christians who adopt this mentality come to realize that most of their time is spent in a world in which God is seen as irrelevant. So, for a couple of hours a week, the Christian enters the church and speaks the language of Christianity. But the rest of the week, the Christian engages the world on its own terms, adopting many of its values and ideas.

This sacred/secular split is damaging to our souls. Ironically, this way of thinking makes our evangelism *less* effective because our lives are no longer seen as the evidence of our proclamation that Jesus Christ is Lord of all. Let's recognize that Jesus is not merely Lord of our religious lives, our evangelistic efforts, and our ministries. He is the King we love and serve, even in our daily jobs.

"The church has nothing to do with politics."

"The church should stay out of politics and just preach the gospel."

"Separation of church and state means that the church should speak to spiritual things, and the state should deal with national things."

"The gospel is politically innocuous."

I hear these types of statements made by a good number of Christians in my own generation. At one level, I understand the sentiments being expressed. Too often, the church has been co-opted by various political causes, and the true gospel has been confused or lost among the competing views. In reaction to this unfortunate reality, people make statements like the ones above.

But it is an overstatement to say that the gospel is politically innocuous. If the apostles were making claims that they considered to be true for all people everywhere, then how can the announcement of a crucified, risen, and now-exalted King be anything *but* political? How is it innocuous to continue to use slogans and titles given to Caesar when preaching about Jesus?

The Gnostics, with their private spiritual experiences, were politically innocuous. But the Christians were thrown to the lions and burned at the stake for being perceived as a threat to Caesar's power.

The church transcends our politics, yet the gospel still has political implications for Christian voters, Christians working in Congress, and even some pastors in what they may preach. The gospel transcends the messages offered by the rulers of the kingdoms of this world by making a declaration about an eternal reality. *Jesus Christ is risen from the dead.* This kind of news affects all spheres of life.

SPOTTING THE COUNTERFEIT
the quietist gospel

STORY	ANNOUNCEMENT	COMMUNITY
The Grand Narrative of Scripture is personal and applicable primarily to those areas of life that we define as spiritual.	Christ's death and resurrection is a private and personal message that changes individual hearts. It is not concerned with society and politics.	The church focuses on self-preservation, maintaining its distinctiveness by resisting the urge to engage prophetically with culture.

Why This Counterfeit Is Attractive

We need to consider why many Christians find the quietist gospel so compelling. It's been said that error comes from "truth out of proportion." This statement proves true of the intentions of many who flirt with this counterfeit. What's true and helpful about the quietist gospel?

It recognizes the danger of the gospel being equated with a political position.

Those with quietist tendencies rightly react against seeing the gospel transformed into a political position and the church being used and abused by powerful people with a political agenda. It doesn't take long to see Jesus co-opted by various groups, whether on the right or the left of the political spectrum. This danger is a constant threat, and the quietist counterfeit is attractive because it recognizes this threat and recoils from it.

It rightly prioritizes personal evangelism as a duty of the church.

Though I don't agree that evangelism is the only duty of a Christian, I agree with those who uphold evangelism as a priority. No matter what we do in our individual vocations to change social structures and laws, or to give bread to the hungry and help to the poor, we should be willing to introduce people to the great Lawgiver, the Bread of Life, and King of the world. If we are not, we fail in fulfilling the Great Commission, which Jesus clearly gave us as our evangelistic mandate.

Countering the Counterfeit

How can we avoid the quietist gospel? We must once more be gripped by the powerful message of the gospel announcement. Just as we expect an individual who has believed the gospel to bear fruit in keeping with the truth, so we expect Christian faithfulness to affect society as we proclaim the truth of Christ's resurrection and lordship.

Demonstrate the gospel in your active concern for the poor and needy.

The gospel is not a message that says, "You should help the poor." The gospel is a message about a sovereign King who gave up heavenly riches in order to humble Himself, die for poor sinners, and then offer them the wealth of His presence forever. Once you are transformed by the gospel announcement of Christ giving His all for needy sinners, your heart goes out to the people around you who have spiritual and temporal needs.

Christ's sacrifice *for you* leads you to sacrifice for others.

According to Jesus, the two great commandments are to love God and to love our neighbor (see Matthew 22:37–39). No matter how much we try, we fail at loving God, and therefore, we fail at loving our neighbor. The good news is that Jesus has fulfilled these two commandments in our place! We no longer stand condemned. United to Jesus Christ, we are declared righteous!

But the good news that Christ has fulfilled this law in our place is not proclaimed to us in order that we might sit back, put our life on cruise control, and head for an eternal destination. The good news that Christ has kept this law in our place and showered us with His grace is *transformative:* it makes us into the kind of people who love God and respond to His mercy by loving our neighbor.

In AD 260, a terrible plague ravished the Roman world. When the sickness took hold in the cities, the pagans sought to escape the confines of the city. As soon as the victims would begin to show symptoms, unbelievers would push the sick away and abandon even their closest family members. Survival became the biggest priority, so much so that suffering people were thrown into the road even before they died. People did anything possible to keep the disease from spreading.

How did the Christians respond to this epidemic? Dionysus gives us a picture that stands in stark contrast to the pagans fleeing the city:

> Most of our brother Christians showed unbounded love and loyalty, never sparing themselves and thinking only of one another. Heedless of danger, they took charge of the sick, attending to their every need and ministering to them in Christ, and with them departed this life serenely happy; for they were infected by others with the disease, drawing on themselves the sickness of their neighbors and cheerfully accepting their pains. Many,

in nursing and curing others, transferred their death to themselves and died in their stead. . . . The best of our brothers lost their lives in this manner, a number of presbyters, deacons, and laymen winning high commendation so that death in this form, the result of great piety and strong faith, seems in every way the equal of martyrdom.[4]

To say that we need only evangelize and not concern ourselves with the poor and suffering is to gut our evangelism of the very actions that demonstrate the truth of our proclamation. The apostle James says that telling a needy brother, "Be warmed and filled," is not enough (James 2:16). That kind of faith is dead. How can we worship a King who became poor on our behalf and yet have no concern for the needy around us?

Bill Wallace was a missionary to China. He loved and served the Chinese people for many years, spanning the events of World War II and the subsequent Communist takeover of the country. He died as a martyr. Wallace was a doctor who used his medical expertise to show compassion and share the gospel. He saw his good works as enhancing the good news he believed and proclaimed.

Wallace wrote: "Every effort has been put forth to fulfill the mission of this hospital. The blind receive their sight and the halt and lame walk; the lepers are cleansed; the deaf hear, the poor have the gospel preached to them. It is our hope and prayer that the medical service in this institution shall be on that high plane befitting the glorious gospel which is preached daily within its walls."[5]

Charles Spurgeon was right to see how Christian compassion and gospel proclamation go together:

Men have enough practical sense always to judge that if professed Christians do not care for their bodily wants, there cannot be much sincerity in their zeal for men's souls. If a man will give me spiritual bread in the form of a tract, but would not give me a piece of bread for my body, how can I think much of him? Let practical help to the poor go with the spiritual help which you render to them. If you would help to keep a brother's soul alive in the higher sense, be not backward to do it in the more ordinary way.[6]

The apostle James tells us that pure and undefiled religion is to "look after orphans and widows in their distress and to keep oneself from being polluted by the world" (James 1:27 NIV). The quietist counterfeit emphasizes personal purity but neglects a Christian's responsibility to the fatherless and the widowed.

The gospel announcement proclaims that we are justified by faith *alone,* but this faith does not come alone. It leads to good works as the fruitful demonstration of the gospel's saving power. That's why Jesus, in Matthew 25, knows the difference between those who merely *say* they know Him and those who actually do. He sees gospel fruit evidenced through our actions of helping those in need.

Here's something to remember: Christians are not benefactors helping the poor. *We* are the ones who are poor. What if God had looked at our spiritual bankruptcy like we look at those who are materially bankrupt? We need to see the poverty of our spiritual state. *We* are the leper outside the camp, the blind beggar on the outskirts of the city, the deaf person needing to hear God's voice. Once we see ourselves in light of God's magnificent grace, God's generosity and grace to us should overflow to those around us.

Maintain a prophetic witness.

My church tradition has a tarnished history when it comes to racism. Fifty years ago, Southern Baptist pastors admirably preached against many forms of worldliness. But there was evil that many pastors never addressed. In small towns throughout

THE QUIETIST GOSPEL ALWAYS ROBS THE CHURCH OF ITS PROPHETIC WITNESS.

the Deep South, outside the comfort of our sanctuaries on a Sunday night, there were African-American brothers whose bodies were swinging from the trees. And many pastors never said a word. The majority of Christians blindly accepted the racial views of their day and never saw the conflict between singing, "Jesus loves the little children, red and yellow, black and white," and silently affirming racism. Our preaching may have been loud, but it was all too quiet.

The quietist gospel always robs the church of its prophetic witness. The liberal version denies the historicity of the gospel announcement and abandons the truth that Christ is the only way to God. By saying, "The gospel is true for me, but not for all," the liberal quietist fails to speak the gospel prophetically in a world in which Christ's exclusive claims are increasingly unpopular.

The conservative version maintains the appearance of prophetic speech by speaking out against certain sins. But it often reduces the gospel announcement by relegating its implications to personal fulfillment in a way that makes the church irrelevant to public discourse. Dietrich Bonhoeffer spoke strongly against this kind of silence: "Flight into the invisible is a denial of the call. A community of Jesus which seeks to hide itself has ceased to follow Him."[7]

Once we lose the public, objective truth-claims at the heart of the gospel announcement, we are bound to falter in our specific mission. Though we should not confuse the gospel with political causes, we fail to take in the cosmic nature of the announcement if we see the gospel as indifferent to injustice in society.

When you proclaim Christ as Savior and Lord, you are demoting all other rivals for His throne. When you exalt Christ as Lord, you are subverting the powers and principalities of this world that hold others in bondage.

D. A. Carson is right: "Because creation gave us embodied existence, and because our ultimate hope is resurrection life in the new heaven and the new earth, we will understand that being reconciled to God and bowing to the lordship of King Jesus cannot possibly be reduced to privatized religion."[8]

The gospel is a word of truth for everyone, including those in power. John the Baptist preached the gospel of the kingdom and called people to repentance. Because he spoke out against the king's immoral lifestyle, he was thrown into prison and later beheaded.

Churches today maintain the public nature of the gospel announcement by both condemning sin in the world and lifting up the gospel that levels us *all*. Lesslie Newbigin has said, "It is a distorted preaching of the gospel which does not lead to fresh commitment to follow Jesus in challenging the domination of evil."[9]

We stand in a long line of courageous men and women who were not afraid to speak out against the injustices of their day. Throughout history, Christians have spoken truth to power.

The saints who went before us were courageous enough to denounce infanticide in ancient Rome and rescue abandoned babies from trash heaps. In England, men like William Wilberforce and John Wesley exposed the horrors of the slave trade and organized Christians into groups that would fight for the rights of people considered to be "inferior." Pastors like Martin Luther King, Jr. have reminded us that every human being bears the image of God regardless of their race. And today, Christians are working to put an end to human trafficking and sexual slavery, and to rid Africa of the scourge of AIDS.

During the rise of the Third Reich, not all the Christians were silent. Dietrich Bonhoeffer was gripped by the gospel of grace. He formed a coalition that stood against Hitler, and eventually, he paid for his resistance with his life. In 1933, he preached a powerful message in which he pleaded with his countrymen to recognize how the true gospel announcement was being overshadowed by nationalism. Bonhoeffer saw that the gospel announcement was being lost, and with it the powerful witness of the gospel community. He urged the churches to return to a strong confession of the lordship of Christ:

> Come you who have been left alone, you who have lost the church, let us return to Holy Writ, let us go forth and seek the church together. . . . For the times, which are times of collapse to the human understanding may well be for her a great time of building. . . . Church, remain a church . . . confess! Confess! Confess![10]

Be missional instead of tribal.

One of the oldest monasteries in the world is Saint Catherine's. Built by Emperor Justinian to protect the monks in the region, St. Catherine's sits at the foot of Mount Sinai in Egypt. The walls are made of granite and are between twenty-six and one hundred fifteen feet (eight and thirty-five meters) tall. Up until last century, there was only one way into the monastery: a tiny door more than thirty feet above the ground. People entered the monastery through a system of pulleys and ropes.

The monastery itself contains ancient icons and many treasures. Until recently, it was largely inaccessible to the outside world.

Our churches naturally drift toward becoming like St. Catherine's monastery: a fortified, doorless organization that focuses on its own preservation rather than its specific mission. Our hearts drift toward tribalism, the tendency to gather with people just like us and to reflect ourselves rather than the missionary heart of God. We're always putting up mirrors around the light of the gospel when we should be putting up windows.

God intends the church to be a colony of heaven, living according to the gospel announcement. The quietist gospel turns the colony into a country club. Our focus becomes the comfort and preservation of our tribe rather than the mission that accompanies the gospel announcement.

I've heard it said that the people of God either have the mentality of a battleship or a cruise ship. Both may sail, but they have very different purposes. The battleship exists for others. It is ready to penetrate the enemy's territory and do battle for the commander. The cruise ship exists for the comfort of its passengers. Luxury and comfort are the core  values, and everyone seeks to make the journey comfortable and memorable.

THE QUIETIST GOSPEL LEADS THE CHURCH TOWARD A CRUISE SHIP MENTALITY.... TO A MESSAGE OF PERSONAL COMFORT.

The quietist gospel leads the church toward a cruise ship mentality. The cross and resurrection of Christ are reduced to a message of personal comfort. Those who embrace the quietist gospel typically make the core value of our worship services a memorable and entertaining experience. Theological debates become about upholding doctrine for doctrine's sake, rather than seeing theological reflection as an aid to fulfilling the mission. Instead of seeing gatherings as a base from which individual Christians scatter into the world as salt and light, quietists wall themselves off from the outside world and neglect the prophetic nature of our gospel announcement.

Tullian Tchividjian explains the difference between a missional and a tribal people:

> The highest value of a community with a tribal mind-set is *self-preservation*. A tribal community exists solely for itself, and

those within it keep asking, "How can we protect ourselves from those who are different from us?

A tribal mind-set is marked by an unbalanced patriotism. It typically elevates personal and cultural preferences to absolute principles: *If everybody were more like us, this world would be a better place.*

But in a missional minded community, the highest value isn't self-preservation but *self-sacrifice.* A missional community exists not primarily for itself but for others. It's a community that's willing to be inconvenienced and discomforted, willing to expend itself for others on God's behalf.[11]

Hold fast to the truthfulness of the gospel announcement.
"Give God a trial run."

"Instead of looking for happiness in these other things, why don't you see if God can be your fix?"

"Jesus came to show us the best possible way to live."

I scratch my head when I hear evangelistic messages that use these and other similar phrases. I'm not sure whether these fit under the category of "therapeutic" or "quietist." The reason I mention them here is because they seem to imply that we call people to faith in Christ primarily because Christianity is helpful. But that is *not* how the apostles make the gospel announcement.

We do not announce the gospel because it is helpful, but because it is true. Helpful or not, *this is the truth about our world.* Newbigin writes: "There can be no true evangelism except that which announces what is not only good news but true news."[12]

When we share the gospel, we are not just inviting people to try a new religious experience. We are proclaiming news about something that has happened. We are proclaiming truth so radical that it turns upside down all notions of what is generally accepted as possible.

Don't minimize the seemingly foolish nature of our gospel.

We are telling people in the twenty-first century to put their faith in a man crucified two thousand years ago, who we say has been actually raised from the dead! The resurrection of Christ is an astounding claim.

Those who say the church needs to "just preach the gospel" are usually thinking of the "gospel" purely in spiritual and personal terms. But the news that Jesus Christ has been raised from the dead can't be contained. Old Testament prophets like Isaiah, Amos, and Ezekiel had no trouble holding together the proclamation of good news with the prophetic call to care for the poor and needy, to stop economically unjust practices, and to return to heartfelt worship of God. John the Baptist and James the apostle told people to repent of their sins, and the two listed *specific sins* that needed to be repented of. Jesus had no trouble revealing the racism between Samaritans and Jews when He told the story of the Good Samaritan.

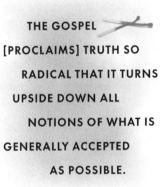

THE GOSPEL [PROCLAIMS] TRUTH SO RADICAL THAT IT TURNS UPSIDE DOWN ALL NOTIONS OF WHAT IS GENERALLY ACCEPTED AS POSSIBLE.

In more recent times, Christians in the South who stayed out of debates about slavery and Jim Crow laws (or, worse, affirmed slavery and racist laws!) were, in effect, privatizing the gospel. Meanwhile missionaries who spoke out against widow-burning in a Hindu context were backing up their gospel proclamation by following their beliefs to their biblical implications.

To put a boundary around this gospel announcement and limit its implications to a person's religious or spiritual life is like trying to contain the fallout of a nuclear explosion in a small box. The gospel announcement nukes our self-righteousness and pride while simultaneously launching a revolution of love that touches every area of our life and all aspects of our society. The gospel births the church, and the church is entrusted with this gospel. When properly announced, the gospel leads to a radical questioning of our society's assumptions.

The gospel leads Christians to be generous to the poor. It leads us to stand up for the oppressed and voiceless. Our hearts break for unborn children murdered in the womb, for young girls sold into a life of sexual slavery, for environmental degradation that puts an end to human flourishing. The gospel announcement is about God's new world crashing into this present age; the story forms us, and the announcement changes us.

The solution to the quietist counterfeit is not to be shrill in our public discourse. Instead, we embrace all the implications of the gospel announcement—especially the fruit of the Spirit, which should characterize our actions—to the point that our churches become a prophetic witness to the gospel.

Light in the Darkness

The Christian church is to stand against the world for the good of the world. Standing against the world may require different postures at different times, but the testimony of the church living according to the public truth of the gospel can be very powerful.

While living in Romania, I often heard stories of what life was like under communism. Villagers would tell me how the constant dread of the securitate (secret police) led them to devise elaborate schemes in order to discover which of their neighbors were informers. The communist leaders were especially hostile toward Christians. Through the years, they sent many students and pastors to prison.

Nicolae Ceausescu rose to power in the 1970s. During his dictatorship, he devastated Romania, plundering the land for natural resources and then exporting so much food that some citizens starved to death. In the 1980s, he dreamed up a nightmarish plan called "systematization." Upon his orders, government officials razed thousands of villages and transferred the country folks to apartment buildings in the cities. These apartments often had no working heat and electricity. Hot water was rationed. So was gasoline, even bread!

I remember hearing of a family who had spent two decades saving money in order to build a new house. No sooner had they built the house than the government seized the property, bulldozed their dream home, and moved the family to a cold, impersonal apartment in the city. The level of injustice in Romanian society was heartbreaking.

But even in the midst of this darkness, the light of the gospel was present in the churches. My father-in-law was a Communist party official sent to spy on a Baptist revival meeting and write down the names of the people who were trusting in Christ. Hearing the gospel, he converted to Christianity and renounced his communist affiliation. At the end of the evening, his own name was on that list!

Other churches also thrived as a countercultural witness during this time. Laszlo Tokes, pastor of the Hungarian Reformed Church in the center of Timisoara, revitalized his church by sharing the gospel with university students. After months of preaching the Word, he began to baptize new converts.

The communists expected churches to eventually become irrelevant. Leaders fanned the quietist tendencies of churches across denominational lines, hoping that preoccupation with a heavenly afterlife would keep Christians from questioning the reigning assumptions of Communist philosophy. Now Tokes's church was threatening the communist dream. The idea that *young* people were embracing the Christian faith posed a threat to those in power.

The securitate threatened church members. They intimidated the pastor and persecuted his family. Finally, a court ordered Tokes to leave his home and be exiled to a small village church. On a Sunday in December, Tokes sadly informed his church that he would be leaving.

Five days later, on December 15, 1989, the securitate came to take Tokes and his wife to the countryside. But they couldn't get into the apartment. Dozens of church members had gathered around his home and would not let the police in. As the evening went on, more and more people passing by joined the protest, lighting candles and singing songs of faith. Other evangelical Christians joined the protest. Eventually, hundreds of candles pierced the darkness of that cold December night.

During the next few days, the number of protestors grew. The secret police eventually used force to remove Tokes and his family, but it was too late. By the time the army fired upon the peaceful protestors, the Romanian Revolution had already begun. Within days, Ceausescu was deposed. By Christmas day, Romania was free.

How did the revolution begin? With a simple pastor and a small church that understood the implications of the gospel announcement. It was the same message that gripped my father-in-law as a young Communist official: "Jesus Christ is Savior and Lord." No matter who might have been in power, there was One with greater power still. And that announcement has repercussions on all of life even today.

Scripture Truths

ON THE CHURCH BEING LIGHT IN SOCIETY: *Psalm 67; Matthew 5:13–16; 28:19; John 17; Acts 1:8*

ON THE CONSEQUENCES OF THE RESURRECTION: *Romans 6:1–14; 8:1–25; 1 Corinthians 15; Ephesians 1:15–20; 6:10–20; Philippians 3:20–21; Colossians 1:15–23; Titus 2:11–14*

ON THE LORDSHIP OF JESUS: *Matthew 28:18; Acts 4:12; Romans 10:9; Philippians 2:10–11*

ON CARING FOR OTHERS: *Matthew 25:31–46; Luke 4:18–19; 5:31–32; 6:20–26; 9:57–58; 10:25–27; 14:12–24; 1 Corinthians 1:26–31; James 1:27; 2:14–17*

PART 3

COMMUNITY

The Truth
the gospel community

A Counterfeit
the activist gospel

A Counterfeit
the churchless gospel

The church is the gospel made visible.

– Mark Dever

the gospel community

HOW DOES a young, Yale-educated atheist find out about evangelical Christians? Gina Welch came up with a plan. She faked a conversion experience, got baptized, and spent two years as a member of Thomas Road Baptist Church in Lynchburg, Virginia. She tells her story in a book called *In the Land of Believers: An Outsider's Extraordinary Journey into the Heart of the Evangelical Church.*

If you're like me, your first reaction upon hearing about a book like this is to roll your eyes and think, *Oh great! An exposé of evangelicals from someone who deliberately engaged in deceptive practices in order to show up evangelical hypocrisy.* But after reading the book for myself, I was pleasantly surprised by Welch's portrayal of evangelicals.

Most intriguing to me were some of the comments Gina makes about the vitality of Christian community. She expresses her longing for the kind of happiness that flows from being part of a church. Writing of her evangelical friends, she says, "They seem to have, as I came to appreciate, a kind of bottomless spring that keeps their happiness lush. I started to believe it was perfectly authentic, and I wanted some for myself."[1]

Then she admits, "What I envied most about Christians was not the God thing—it was having a community gathering each week, a touchstone for people who share values, a safe place to be frank about your life struggles, a place to be reminded of your moral compass. Having a place to guard against loneliness, to feel there are others like you."[2]

Sadly, though Gina sensed the power of Christian community, she chose to remain an outsider looking in. But her story reminds us that there is something special about a community of faith gathering to worship the crucified and risen Lord Jesus. Even an unbeliever can sense the power of the gospel community.

The Gospel Announcement Births the Church

We've looked at the first two legs of the three-legged stool that represents the gospel. We've seen how *the gospel story* is the context in which we make *the gospel announcement*. But we must not neglect the third leg of this stool, *the gospel community* that the announcement births.

Too many times, we evangelicals miss the full picture of the gospel by telling a story that goes something like this: *God loves you, but you have sinned against Him. You need redemption, which is provided by Jesus Christ, who died for your sins. If you accept Jesus, your relationship with God will be restored and you will live in heaven with Him after you die.*

There is nothing untrue about any of these statements. But this presentation has reduced the great story of the Bible to a message about me and God. And that message simply doesn't do justice to what we see in the Bible. Ask yourself, Why does the

Bible tell us the story of Israel? Why are there so many letters given to the church? Why do we have all the laws that were to govern God's people in their common life together? Why does God make a covenant with David? Why does the Bible contain the prophets' messages to the people of God?

The answer is this: God desires to care for and mature a chosen community of people. The story of the Bible tracks the journey of God's covenant community, a people commissioned to be salt and light for the good of this world and the glory of God's name. The focus of the Bible (and the focus of God's saving work) is His beloved community: ethnic Israel in the Old Testament and the true Israel (Jew and Gentile alike who profess faith in Christ) in the New Testament. Joshua Harris writes:

> God's plan for glorifying himself in the world has always been a group plan. He has always planned to redeem a *people*. And he's always revealed himself to the world through a nation. That was the past perfection in the first pages of the book of Genesis. That is the future described in the closing pages of Revelation—God dwelling among his people.[3]

The gospel story and the gospel announcement lead to the formation of the gospel community. The church is not an afterthought in the purposes of God. Pastors Tim Chester and Steve Timmis are right: "The church . . . is not something additional or optional. It is at the very heart of God's purposes. Jesus came to create a people who would model what it means to live under His rule. It would be a glorious outpost of the kingdom of God, an embassy of heaven. This is where the world can see what it means to be truly human."[4] The gospel announcement births people into God's kingdom, and God makes His kingdom visible through the formation of His church.

What Is the Church?

Sometimes you'll hear people use the term "universal church." The universal church refers to all the redeemed of all the ages. But most of the time, the Scriptures speak of the church as a "local church." The local church is a visible manifestation of the invisible, universal church.

The actual word "church" can be translated as "assembly." A local church is a group of believers in Jesus Christ who gather together to fulfill the functions of the church, which include worship, prayer, fellowship, evangelism, service, and discipleship.

The church's corporate identity witnesses to the coming kingdom of God. You may have heard the phrase "Stake out the land." This goes back to explorers who had come across lands yet undiscovered. By putting a stake in the ground, the explorers were claiming the land for the kingdom they represented. A church is like a stake in the ground, an outpost that by its very existence declares, "God is king here."

As witnesses to the kingdom of God, church members proclaim the gospel. We proclaim the gospel individually by engaging in personal evangelism and calling others to repentance. We proclaim the gospel corporately by gathering to hear the Word of God preached in our midst.

Churches also proclaim the gospel by observing the sacraments: baptism and the Lord's Supper. When churches baptize believers, we proclaim (in signs) the gospel of Christ's burial and resurrection. When churches partake of the Lord's Supper, we are putting on display the gospel of Christ's broken body for sinners' redemption. As we serve one another, others know we are Christians by our love.

J. I. Packer has summed up our mission this way: "The task of the church is to make the invisible kingdom visible through faithful Christian living and witness-bearing."[5]

So how do we rightly understand the gospel community?

How do we keep from leading people to believe a gospel announcement that fails to incorporate them into a local congregation? There are four truths related to the church that we should consider.

Truth 1: The Church Embodies the Gospel

The church is an embodiment of the gospel message. God's plan from the very beginning has been to spotlight His glory by redeeming a people who submit to His rule. Our lives together make the gospel visible.

Joining a church is not an optional good work for some Christians. The local church is the place where we put into action all that we believe. Our beliefs about God, about ourselves, about Jesus Christ, and about repentance and faith—these beliefs are fleshed out and made visible by our life in the church. Mark Dever says: "God is displaying, lighting up His gospel, through our churches."[6]

The Witness of Our Life Together

How do unbelievers know we are Christians? By the fish symbols on our car? By our bumper stickers? By our voting patterns? By our church attendance? No, Jesus tells us that the outside world will know we are Christians by the way we love one another (see John 13:34–35; 1 John 4:12). When we submit to one another in love, we bolster our evangelistic witness by showing the world that love and authority don't have to be separated. God's rule is life-giving. He rules us for our good and for His glory, and the church reflects that loving rule.

If you want to witness effectively to the gospel, invite people to observe the community of faith. Let them witness our common life together. Let them see the basic themes of the gospel announcement by the way we treat one another.

Since God has forgiven us through the costly blood of His Son, so must we pour ourselves out to others in love and forgiveness. As we have received forgiveness, we grant forgiveness. As God keeps His promises to us, so we keep our promises to those in our church. Remembering that God has laid down His life for His enemies, we commit to telling the truth no matter the personal cost. Since God has cared for us, we care for each other. Since God has conquered evil on our behalf, we stand for the oppressed and the persecuted. And those outside the community watch and know there is a genuine difference.

A Community Birthed by the Gospel

When I use the term "gospel community," I mean "the community birthed by the gospel announcement." The church is not the good news. We announce the gospel within the context of its story. But we are only witnesses to the gospel, not the gospel itself.

Our good deeds are a sweet fragrance to the God who has redeemed us, but our works are not the gospel. So when Christian activists tell us, "We are the ones we've been waiting for," we must respectfully disagree. The church is not the gospel, but the gospel does form the church. Our communal life together is intended to be a display of the good news for a watching world.

Truth 2: The Gospel Incorporates Us into a Community of Faith

The New Testament uses many metaphors when describing the gospel community. We are called a "flock" (Acts 20:28). We are said to be the body of Christ with Christ as the head (1 Corinthians 12:12). There is also a picture of the church as a building (1 Peter 2:5). Notice how these metaphors incorporate us as individuals into the congregation as a whole. Each of us takes our place within the community, as a sheep in the flock, as a member of the body, as a living stone in the house.

When we rightly understand the story being told in the Scriptures, we see how much God invests in forming communities that reflect His glory. In the Old Testament, God calls out the people of Israel. In the New Testament, He sets about calling people from every tribe, tongue, and nation to believe in His Son. The gospel announcement is intended to incorporate us into a community of faith.

Baptized into one Body

Remember God's promise to deliver the children of Israel out of the hands of an oppressive Egyptian pharaoh? God tells them, "I will take you to be my people, and I will be your God, and you shall know that I am the Lord your God, who has brought you out from under the burdens of the Egyptians" (Exodus 6:7). God promises rescue in order to prove His love for them. They will be His *people.* In Deuteronomy 4:20, Moses says, "The Lord has taken you and brought you out of the iron furnace, out of Egypt, to be a people of His own inheritance, as you are this day." God saved every single Hebrew from slavery in order that they might *together* be the people of His own inheritance.

The same theme runs through the New Testament. In the Gospels, we see that during the week of Passover, Jesus went to the cross to pay the price for our sins. If the purpose of Christ's atoning death was merely to make atonement for individuals, He might have chosen the Day of the Atonement, Yom Kippur, the day when the priest made atonement for sin. Instead, it appears that Jesus chose Passover because of its corporate significance. The atoning death (the blood of the lamb smeared on the doorposts) leads to the rescue of the community (the Exodus), in order that the people may freely worship God and reflect His glory.[7]

In one of Paul's letters, we read, "For just as the body is one and has many members, and all the members of the body, though many, are one body, so it is with Christ. For in one Spirit we were all baptized into one body—Jews or Greeks, slaves or free—and all were made to drink of one Spirit" (1 Corinthians 12:12–13). We are not baptized as individual Christians out there in the world. We are baptized *into a community.*

John Stott reminds us of the Holy Spirit's work in the early church: "He 'added to their number . . . those who were being saved.' He didn't add them to the church without saving them, and he didn't save them without adding them to the church. Salvation and church membership went together; they still do."[8]

The gospel incorporates us into a family. Justification by faith has two dimensions: a saving dimension (in which we are declared righteous because of Christ's obedient life and sacrificial death in our place) and a corporate dimension (in which we are united to those whose faith in Christ becomes their primary identity). Joseph Hellerman puts it this way: We are justified and then "familified"—adopted into God's family.[9] There is a vertical aspect to our justification (we are reconciled to God), which then leads to a horizontal dimension (we are reconciled to one another).

For Me, for Us, for God

A few years ago, I volunteered to be a counselor at a youth camp. During the bus ride to camp, I had a conversation with one of the other counselors. She told me the story of how she came to faith in Christ. "I grew up going to Catholic school and church," she said. "I knew who Jesus was. I had an awe and fear of God instilled in me. I believed that Jesus Christ died on the cross for the sins of the world."

Then she stopped, her lip quivering. "But I never really understood that Jesus died *for me.*" She went on to tell me about how she attended a Christian concert where she heard the message of the gospel. All of her Christian knowledge about Jesus became personal. Her heart was captured by the glorious truth that Christ died *for her.* Martin Luther made much of the phrase "for me," and rightly so. That phrase is at the heart of the Reformation, for God's personal love for us penetrates our hard hearts and brings lasting change.

Interestingly enough, the summer in which I listened to this woman's testimony was the summer in which I was having an epiphany that went the opposite way. Having grown up in evangelical churches all my life, I had always taken for granted the truth that Christ died *for me.* That truth was emphasized again and again, and it had gripped my heart long ago. What was becoming more glorious to me was the truth that Christ died *for us.* I was beginning to see in Scripture how Christ's death purchased His church as a bride. Furthermore, this action *for us* was ultimately *for God and His glory.* My epiphany was grasping the truth that Christ's death *for me* was bigger and better than I had ever dreamed: it was also *for us* and *for God.*

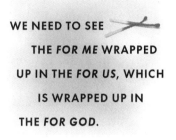

WE NEED TO SEE THE *FOR ME* WRAPPED UP IN THE *FOR US,* WHICH IS WRAPPED UP IN THE *FOR GOD.*

I'm afraid we often take the glorious *for me* of the gospel and separate it from the *for us* and the *for God.* We shrink the gospel down until it is a message about the individual standing before God that no longer contains the gospel community at the heart of God's plan. Instead, we need to see the *for me* wrapped up in the *for us,* which is wrapped up in the *for God.* It all goes back to God and His glory being made manifest through the church that he has bought with the blood of His Son.

Emphasize the *for me* to the exclusion of everything else, and you wind up with an individualistic message about personal salvation; the church becomes an optional side-effect of the gospel message. Emphasize the *for us* and *for God* aspects of the message and you never bring the good news down to the personal level; you don't challenge someone to trust in Christ. But put them together, and you have the biblical understanding of the gospel—both individual and corporate. Once you grasp all three aspects, your personal salvation story is given eternal significance because it is caught up in the great, unfolding drama dreamed up in the heart of our good and loving Creator.

Truth 3: The Gospel Community Is Made Up of Kingdom People

Picture an old church building. The church's steeple stands against a blue sky. Worn from years of wind and rain, the building's exterior reveals its age. The doors are open, but only for tourists interested in the architecture. Floors creak; dust sits on the pews. Once the platform for Bible preaching, the altar is only a museum curiosity, untouchable in a glass case.

The most unusual aspect of this museum-church is the cemetery outside. You think to yourself, *Surely, we twenty-first-century Christians are too sophisticated to pass by a graveyard on our way into church every Sunday. Only morbid fascination could have led Christian saints to bury their dead so close to the house of worship.*

Yet the gravestones tell another story. "With Jesus, I shall rise," says one. "The grave cannot confine me here. When Christ doth call, I must appear!" says another. "I know that my Redeemer lives," affirms a third. Preoccupation with death doesn't explain the cemetery's strange location. Instead, it was the church's anticipation of new life. The tombstones reveal the joyous truth: Resurrection is coming! Death has lost its sting. God's promises of new heaven and earth will soon be fulfilled.

Resurrection People

Teaching on the final resurrection "passed away" long ago in most evangelical circles. Whenever we mention rising from the dead, we almost always reference Jesus' resurrection. Sadly, we forget the link that connects Jesus' rising to our own. When we lose sight of our future resurrection, the Easter message loses power and relevance. We also lose our understanding of the power of the church's presence on earth right now.

When the disciples saw the risen Jesus, they sensed He was in a position to initiate His earthly kingdom—though as Acts 1:6–8 shows, they were confused about when that would come to pass. Jesus' resurrection was the event that marked the beginning of God's new world and gave them hope that God would one day vindicate all His chosen people by reversing the curse of death, raising them bodily from the dead, and giving them eternal, incorruptible, and transformed bodies. Though the old age of sin and decay continued on, the new age had begun.

THE FINAL DWELLING PLACE OF GOD IS TO COME FROM HEAVEN TO BE WITH MAN.

The Bible teaches that the Messiah's past is our future. Jesus' resurrection is the foretaste—the firstfruits—of the resurrection in which all Christians will one day share (1 Corinthians 15:20). What is true of our Messiah will be true of us (2 Timothy 2:11).

The final resurrection reminds us that the Christian's hope is much richer than a disembodied heavenly experience after death. What we usually call "heaven" is what the New Testament writers would have considered an intermediary state—a holding place for the saved until the resurrection of the Last Day.[10] Don't think, though, that this "paradise" was just a place for "soul sleep." Paul proclaimed that to be "absent from the body [was] to be present with the Lord" (2 Corinthians 5:8 KJV). Nonetheless, as nice as the temporary afterlife may be, the apostles saw it as simply a stop on the way to the glorious new heaven and earth that God had promised to bring about.

We often miss the big picture because we gloss over the Bible passages that speak continually about life *after* the afterlife—the promised new heaven and earth. We are like travelers on our way to the Grand Canyon, giving all our attention to the Hilton we'll be resting at overnight on the journey. As nice as the Hilton may be, it is only a stop on the path to the splendor ahead.

The biblical view of the afterlife is not about escaping earth to get to heaven. It's about heaven coming on earth—the New Jerusalem coming from God's dimension onto a physical newly created and transformed earth (Revelation 21:2). It's not about *shedding* our bodies; it's about God *transforming* them into an incorruptible state (2 Corinthians 5:2–4). The final dwelling place of man is not to go to heaven to be with God; the final dwelling place of God is to come from heaven to be with man (Revelation 21:3–4).

Cemeteries once surrounded churches because the saints knew that the coffins they nailed shut would one day be thrown open. The decayed and dusty remains of a once-vibrant body would be transformed into a new type of physical reality—one that will never know death. Believers wanted to be near their church house when the trumpet sounds.

The tombstones continue to speak: "My flesh shall slumber in the ground, 'till the last of trumpets joyful sound. Then burst the chains with sweet surprise, and in my Savior's image rise!" Another simply says, "Waiting." Curiously, the more recent the gravestones, the fewer the references to the Christian's glorious hope. The church must have moved away from speaking on the resurrection. Suddenly, you begin to wonder, *Maybe that's what turned the church into a museum.*

Kingdom Colonizers

The church on earth agrees with the apostle Peter's confession that Jesus Christ is the messiah king. The apostle Paul says that we are citizens of heaven. Many times we think of our heavenly citizenship in terms of how our home is elsewhere. But this is not the proper understanding of a colony.

We often hear phrases like, "Heaven is my home; this earth is just a temporary stopping point." Biblically, that picture is backwards. Christians who die go to heaven with a round-trip ticket. Our final destination is a new *earth*—the place where righteousness dwells (2 Peter 3:13). Those who have gone before us are already in the presence of the Lord, but even they wait with anticipation for the resurrection of their bodies and the final restoration of all things.

We were not made for heaven; we were made for earth. Specifically, we were made for heaven *on* earth. The church is a colony of the coming kingdom. When the pilgrims came to the new world and established (eventually) thirteen colonies, they had no intention of staying here for a long time and then returning to England, their true home. They realized that the new world was their home, and they did everything they could to make sure that the best of British culture made it here. They colonized America for the motherland.

Likewise, we live according to the gospel announcement as ambassadors for the true King. Our faithful presence here on earth should provide a glimpse of what the life of heaven is like. We are to be a fragrance of the new world that is coming and a warning of the accompanying judgment. The church is the society where the kingdom of Jesus Christ is manifested and extended.

Let's say that you live in a town that is in a desert. One day, someone shows up and says, "Get ready for snowfall! A north wind will come and bring snow that will cover this land. The world will be like new, but you must be prepared for the day it snows!" Even though you live in a town that has never seen snow, people believe the strange message that snow will fall and blanket the town.

The people who believe in the coming snow begin to prepare the town for Christmas. Some put up Christmas lights. Others design snow plows. Still others cover their plants. Even if most people scoff at the snow-watchers, the group maintains their belief that everything will be made new. And mysteriously, whenever the snow people come together, a cool breeze begins to blow and it flurries just a bit, giving them just a taste of the glory that's coming.

The church of Jesus Christ is like a flurry before the great snow. Christians live in light of the coming reality. When we gather together, we sense the Spirit of God blowing through our midst, changing us and renewing the world around us. We also warn people of the judgment that will accompany the presence of God on that day. We are a colony of heaven, and our life together makes the announcement: *Repent, trust in the Messiah-King who has died for your sins, and be ready for the coming kingdom!*

United at the Foot of the Cross

During the Rwandan genocide in the mid 1990s, there was a school that had teenage students from both the Hutu and Tutsi tribes. One day, three men burst into the school with guns and a machete. The students were terrified. One of the men shouted: "I want you to separate yourselves between Hutu and Tutsi."

One of the boys in the room, Phanuel, worried about what might take place. Catherine Claire Larson, author of *As We Forgive*, described what happened next. Phanuel:

> "felt like his heart would beat out of his chest. As a Hutu, he knew that he could say something and perhaps spare his life, but he couldn't imagine betraying his own friends. He knew also that as a Christian he didn't have that option. He prayed, "Lord, help us." It couldn't have been more than a few moments that the rebel waited for an answer, but to Phanuel it seemed like time had slowed. And then there was a voice. Phanuel winced.
>
> "All of us are Rwandans here," said Chantal from the front of the classroom. A shot rang out in reply. The students gasped—

the bullet hit Chantal squarely in the forehead.

"Hutu here! Tutsi there!" yelled the man . . . "This is your last chance. You will separate or you will all die."

Just then Emmanuel said in a steady, low voice, "We are all Rwandans." Shots punctuated Emmanuel's statement as the men moved their guns systematically across the room.[11]

Many of the students perished. But none of them betrayed the others.

The solidarity of the Hutu and Tutsi students reflects the kind of solidarity that should be ours in the church. We are not black or white, rich or poor, Jew or Gentile, slave or free, male or female. We are one in Christ Jesus. Our gatherings should boldly proclaim, "All of us are Christians here!"

Our life together as a community should reflect the coming kingdom. As much as possible, we should seek to unite races and social classes, nationalities and ethnicities, cultures and backgrounds—all around the cross of Christ and our common desire to remain faithful to him.

John Newton, the composer of "Amazing Grace," held a high social status in his day. But the grace of God that changed him from a slave-trader to a pastor was the same grace that caused him to bridge class divisions in his church ministry. "Preferring his old blue captain's jacket over 'proper' clerical garb, he hobnobbed with spiritually alive folks wherever he found them, regardless of their social status. He once wrote, 'I get more warmth and light sometimes by a letter from a plain person who loves the Lord Jesus, though perhaps a servant maid, than from some whole volumes put forth by learned doctors.'"[12]

This kind of unity among Christians is one way that the church can reflect the centrality of the cross. By uniting around the death and resurrection of Jesus, we show the world the power of the gospel announcement displayed through the gospel community.

Truth 4: The Gospel Community Is the Place Where We Are Sanctified

While I was in seminary, I worked at a local restaurant. On one occasion, I invited a co-worker to come to church with me. She waved me off, saying, "The church is full of hypocrites!"

To her surprise, I agreed. "Yes, it is," I said, and then added with a smile, "so you'd fit right in with us. We're all hypocrites to some extent, aren't we?"

She had never thought of herself as a hypocrite, but she started to nod and then said, "I think you're right."

Then I asked, "Is there anyone you've known *who really did walk the walk?*" She started to talk about her grandmother and the godly testimony she had. Pretty soon, she was no longer comparing herself to the hypocritical church members she looked down on; she was comparing herself to a godly woman.

> THE CHURCH, FOR ALL ITS FAILURES, IS WHERE WE LOVE ONE ANOTHER . . . AND STIR UP EACH OTHER.

It's become fashionable lately to make fun of the church. I understand that the church has major flaws and deficiencies. It's been said that the church of Jesus Christ is like Noah's ark. The stench inside would be unbearable if it weren't for the storm outside! But my question to those who want to leave it is this: *Where else will you be able to submit to loving authority? Where else will God sanctify you?* The church, for all its failures, is where we love one another, bear with one another, and stir up each other's affections for good deeds.

The good news of the gospel is not merely that God saves us by grace; it's that this saving grace transforms our lives in the context of a community. We bind ourselves to other Christians in faithfulness to a common confession of faith in our Lord. We affirm the truth of the gospel together. We commit to one another: comforting, rebuking, challenging, and loving.

The church exists primarily for God's glory, but it also exists for our good. We need the church to help us discover our gifts so we can best serve the body of believers. We need the church to affirm the evidence in our lives that Christ has saved us through His grace. We need the church to re-present the gospel through baptism and the Lord's Supper. We need the church to rebuke and challenge us when we are wandering from the narrow path.

Discipleship is like a rock in a rock tumbler. The rock is shined the more it bumps up against all the other rocks and water. Over time, the process turns a rock into a gem. Discipleship requires community. The church is the place where we are shaped by the living water of Jesus and the presence of other Christians (living stones) until we turn into beautiful gems that reflect the glory of our King.

Dietrich Bonhoeffer wrote about community:

> When God had mercy on us, when God revealed Jesus Christ to us as our brother, when God won our hearts by God's own love, our instruction in Christian love began at the same time. When God was merciful to us, we learned to be merciful with one another. When we received forgiveness instead of judgment, we too were made ready to forgive each other. What God did to us, we then owed to others. The more we received, the more we were able to give; and the more meager our love for one another, the less we were living by God's mercy and love. Thus God taught us to encounter one another as God has encountered us in Christ. "Welcome one another, therefore, just as Christ has welcomed you, for the glory of God" (Romans 15:7).[13]

For the Glory of God and the Good of the World

God chooses to funnel His grace and mercy through us to the wider community of faith, and through the community's witness to the outer world. The church does not exist for itself; it exists for the mission of God. Our life together magnifies the glory of God.

Once we are gripped by the gospel of grace, we are filled with gratitude for the Son of God who made Himself nothing, took the form of a servant, and humbled Himself even to death on a cross. Our lives take on the fragrance of forgiveness. Pride is replaced by humility. Our rush to the front of the line is turned into a rush to find a place to serve. Our brashness is replaced by gentleness. The cross shapes us into the image of the Crucified One.

The gospel community is empowered by the Holy Spirit to be a blessing to the nations by bringing the good news of salvation and living distinctly from the world for the good of the world.

Scripture Truths

ON THE CHURCH'S FOUNDATION: *Matthew 16:13–19; 1 Corinthians 3:11; Ephesians 2:20*

ON THE CHURCH AS CHRIST'S BODY: *Romans 12:4–8; Ephesians 1:20–23; Colossians 1:18; 1 Corinthians 12:12–27*

ON THE CHURCH AS A COLONY OF THE KINGDOM: *Matthew 18:20; Colossians 1:12; 3:1–4; Philippians 3:19–20*

ON SANCTIFICATION: *John 14:15; Romans 6:4; 8:13; 12:1; 13:4; 12–14; 2 Corinthians 3:18; 5:17; Galatians 5:16–17; Colossians 3:8–10; Philippians 2:12–13; 1 Peter 1:15–16; 1 John 3:2*

*Our generation is prone to radicalism
without follow-through. We want to change the world
and we have never changed a diaper.*

– Kevin DeYoung

the activist gospel

A FRIEND of mine once told me about a little Kentucky church concerned about a city council proposal that would allow local businesses to sell alcohol. For years, the county had been "dry." Because the church members had witnessed the damage caused by alcohol abuse, they wanted to protect their neighbors and families from temptation. So they decided to act.

For a period of several months, the little church became the headquarters of the anti-alcohol movement. Church members knocked on doors and asked people to vote against the new proposal. They put out signs, organized volunteers, took up offerings, and sent out mailers.

On the day of the crucial vote, the church members gathered in their sanctuary around the radio, breathlessly awaiting the results of all their efforts. After a couple of hours, the news came in. The church had won. The proposal to allow the sale of alcohol in the county had been defeated. The church members cheered. Whoops and hollers echoed throughout the sanctuary. Hugs were exchanged and beverages were passed around (non-alcoholic, of course). One of the deacons turned to my friend and said, "This is the *best day* our church has ever had."

When my friend told me that a deacon called it "the best day," I wondered. *Really*? Regardless of one's views on alcohol consumption, does it not seem sad that a church would view the passing of legislation as the greatest event in its history? What about the day someone's grandson walked down the aisle asking to be baptized? What about the day when the church gathered for the funeral of a charter member, and several of her family members trusted Christ? What about when the church commissioned a missionary family who left the small Kentucky town to go to the ends of the earth with the gospel? No, in this little country church some members had become so enthralled with their activism that they imagined the angels rejoicing in heaven over one proposition voted down by the constituents.

The Activist Gospel

No church, whether conservative or liberal, liturgical or contemporary, big or small, is immune to the appeal of the activist gospel. Evangelicals, perhaps more than other segments of Christianity, are especially tempted by this counterfeit because we are a people of action. We want to see Christ's kingdom advanced. But the activist counterfeit is detrimental to the gospel, particularly the gospel community, because it unites us around social action or political causes rather than the gospel itself.

In an earlier chapter, we saw that the gospel is public news that has implications for all of society, including the business world, art, literature, science, and politics. The danger of the quietist gospel is that its message is sealed off from our public life. The quietist counterfeit is like throwing a rock into a lake and trying to contain the ripple effect.

The activist gospel makes the opposite mistake, focusing on the ripples that come from the gospel announcement rather than the rock itself. This counterfeit unites the gospel community around a common cause instead of our common Christ. Once the cause becomes the driving force of the church, the Great Commission is supplanted, worship of God and observing the sacraments are downplayed, and the church becomes a social institution that—in the attempt to be prophetic and powerful—loses its voice in the midst of competing ideologies.

Evangelical Versions of the Activist Gospel

How does the activist gospel seep into our churches? Here are three ways that the gospel can eventually be supplanted by our work:

Culture Warriors

There is a battle of ideas in our society today. Some have likened this battle of ideas to a war. Our culture continues its move toward secularization and relativism as traditional morality degenerates in our neighborhoods, schools, and even our churches. Evangelicals are encouraged to stand up and fight for traditional values and for the recognition of God in society.

The problem with the culture warrior mind-set is that it confuses the church and culture. So while pastors speak out against sins like adultery in society, the church overlooks the adulterer still singing from the choir loft. We want the Ten Commandments in the courthouse, but we can't list the Ten Commandments when asked.

Not long ago, commentator Glenn Beck had a prominent evangelical join him on his TV show. When speaking about the difference between Beck's Mormonism and evangelical theology, the evangelical said, "We can argue about theology later, after we save the country." This is the culture warrior mind-set in a nutshell. We believe we are in a battle in which the righteous oppose the unrighteous. The inevitable result is a feeling of hostility toward non-Christians who differ with us on political issues. Russell Moore has reminded evangelicals who the real enemy is: "We should rage against the reptile and not against his prey."[1]

The culture war moves us in the opposite direction from the cross. Instead of laying down our lives for others in love, by serving our opponents and demonstrating charity in our speech and actions, we begin to look down on those around us. The activist gospel changes our posture toward the world. We no longer see ourselves as having been rescued by the grace of God for His glory and the good of our neighbors. Instead, we feel it is our duty to rescue the world from its path to destruction, and we blow past anyone who might get in our way.

Errand Runners

In reaction to much of the rhetoric of the conservative culture warriors, many younger evangelicals have embraced different areas of activism. Instead of fighting abortion or same-sex marriage, they promote environmentalism, relief for the poor, and social justice. The goal? Make the world a better place. Unfortunately, this group also loses its prophetic voice and becomes just another interest group. We become "errand runners." Others set the agenda. We just run errands for the world.

To be fair, the errand runners recognize that injustice needs to be challenged. But the undergirding assumption that unites both the culture warriors and the errand runners is this: *Politics and policy are where the real change occurs.* So whether you are a right-wing activist or a left-wing activist, you're united by your belief that politics is the primary way of changing the world.

The Educators

There is a third variation of the activist gospel, and this group may be either culture warriors or errand runners. They are the educators. Since the main problem of society is said to be ignorance, the solution is education. Crime and poverty and unemployment and all the other woes of our culture will be solved if we can improve people's education.

Certainly, Christians have been on the front lines of increasing educational opportunities. From promoting literacy in the days of the Reformation to helping immigrants learn English today, Christians are right to see education as an integral part of building a society for the common good.

But education—as good as it is—should never supplant the gospel. Our biggest problem is not our ignorance, but our rebellion against God. To treat the human heart as if it is basically good and merely needing direction is to make a fundamental misdiagnosis of our condition. Education makes us smarter sinners, but it does not address the heart.

Co-opting Jesus Today

Everyone wants Jesus to be on their side. I've heard culture warriors who uphold the Second Amendment right to own guns cite Jesus as their example. A recent Bible translation project called "the Conservative Project" rejects and rewrites any verse that may bolster the views of those who are politically liberal. Thankfully, this project has received scorn from those on the right and the left.

The errand runners co-opt Jesus too. Jesus turns out to be a peace-loving hippie. We ask questions like "What would Jesus drive?" This group often leaves aside the harsh words of Christ, not to mention Revelation's picture of Christ's return in blazing, warrior-like glory.

The educators also co-opt Jesus, turning Him into a great teacher, but not much of a Savior. Their idea is that following the principles of Christ would make this world a better place. All we need to do is teach others what Jesus taught. Let's love one another and try to get along!

Co-opting Jesus in His Day

Our current efforts to make Jesus the patron saint of our favorite cause is nothing new. Even in Jesus' time, there were groups that initially would have loved to claim Him, and yet they despised Him for the ways He did not fit their agenda.

The Pharisees were the conservative stream of Judaism in their day. They sought to be faithful to the Law of Moses by making it practical for their daily lives. They tried to live at peace with the Romans who oppressed them. But Jesus was not a Pharisee. He decried their hypocrisy and would not play by the rules they invented.

The Zealots were another group in Jesus' world. They advocated a violent overthrow of the Roman government. Zealots were intrigued by Jesus' talk about being Messiah, and some would have loved for him to lead a revolution. But Jesus spoke of taking up the cross, going the extra mile, and loving the Roman enemy. He would not be taken in by their cause and their desire for political revolution. The cross would be His throne.

The Sadducees were theological sell-outs. They had abandoned belief in the resurrection on the last day. Many of them were cultural Jews, profiting from the Jewish sacrificial system. But they were primarily interested in maintaining their reputation with the ruling elite and the Roman oppressors. Jesus condemned the Sadducees for abandoning the Word of God and mocking God's power.

The Essenes were the monastic movement of Jesus' day. They had disappeared into the wilderness, believing that Israel must be purified before God's rescue could take place. So they devoted themselves to purity out in the desert, hoping that God would intervene in the plight of their people. Jesus preached like an Essene on occasion, and He frequently went out into desolate places to be alone, but He was not a part of their group. He said that light should be shined before others, not hidden under a bowl.

Salt must be in the world for its saltiness to be effective.

Jesus was no Pharisee, Zealot, Sadducee, or Essene. He was who He was. He is who He is. And try as hard as we may, we cannot fit Jesus into our pet causes and stereotypes either. He will break out of any box we put Him in. He cannot be tamed. That's why we are told to seek first His kingdom, not the passing kingdoms and towers of Babel we build in this world.

SPOTTING THE COUNTERFEIT
the activist gospel

STORY	ANNOUNCEMENT	COMMUNITY
The kingdom is advanced through the efforts of Christians to build a just society. We are the answer to our prayers for a better world.	The gospel's power is demonstrated through political, social and cultural transformation brought about by involved Christians.	The church finds its greatest unity around political causes or social projects.

Why This Counterfeit Is Attractive

There are various reasons why we are attracted to the activist gospel. Here are three common ones:

The activist gospel makes a difference in society.

This counterfeit is attractive because the biblical gospel *will* lead us to make a difference in society. We should be known for being pro-life, helping the poor, building schools, digging wells, and promoting literacy. We should be the ones who courageously speak against injustice in its many forms. The activist gospel is right to insist that Christianity is about the real world, not a private spiritual world of retreat.

The activist gospel brings immediate results.

The activist gospel promises that a difference can be made *now*. Pass legislation, and you see immediate results. Dig a well in Africa, and you provide fresh water for a village. Show a pregnant woman an ultrasound, and she will probably keep her baby. We want to see change take place quickly. Good results fuel our desire to stay active.

Let's face it. Sometimes, making disciples is tiresome. We pour our lives into others, only to be disappointed. The common, week-in and week-out routine of hearing the Word and celebrating the Lord's Supper can become dull, no matter how many ways we try to keep it fresh. The activist gospel is attractive because it promises immediate results in tangible ways.

The activist gospel makes us popular with people we want to impress.

The activist gospel can make you popular. Culture warriors know that their positions will be unpopular with many in the world. But their positions bring popularity from church members who enjoy the fight.

Errand runners want to be countercultural, but the culture they are countering is the culture-warrior mind-set of their churches. Taking on issues like social justice and environmentalism brings applause and affirmation from the people outside their circles. Amy Sullivan, writing for *Time* magazine notices that much of the young evangelical move to fight poverty is simply because it's popular. She asks, "If a movement is based on popularity, the inevitable question has to be asked: 'What happens to the cause when it's not popular anymore?' It's hard to sustain anything long-term if it's based merely on popularity."[2]

Countering the Counterfeit

How can we be salt and light in our world without falling for the activist gospel that supplants the biblical gospel with our own efforts of changing the world? Here are some suggestions:

Don't confuse the gospel with the effects of the gospel.

The word "gospel" means "good news." It is news that must be proclaimed. Christians are heralds of this gospel, telling the world that something has happened. Since the content of the gospel announcement is about what God has done through Jesus Christ to reconcile us to Him and to bring restoration to the world, we must remember that this news is not about what we do. It is about what Christ has done.

THE COMMUNITY BIRTHED BY THE GOSPEL WILL PERFORM ALL SORTS OF GOOD DEEDS . . . [BUT] OUR WORK IS NOT THE GOSPEL.

I fear that many of the good activities that Christians are involved in, whether opposing abortion, fighting poverty, promoting peace, or tutoring young people in failing schools (activities in which I have also taken part) are sometimes thought of as spreading the gospel. We should never describe our good deeds as "gospel proclamation." The gospel is what *drives* our good deeds, not the story of those good deeds.

When the gospel announcement is properly made within the gospel story, the community that is birthed by the gospel will perform all sorts of good deeds. Christians will be involved in various spheres of public life, bringing their Christian convictions to their places of vocation and influence. Once our hearts are made new, once we are changed by the gospel, we inevitably become agents of change in the places where God has planned for us to be.

Nevertheless, our work is not *the gospel*. Rob Bell, in his moving Nooma video "You," uses a symphony to show how the church works together for the common good. But Rob is mistaken when he looks into the camera and tells the audience, "You are the gospel." That kind of statement leads to a confusion of our good works and the gospel announcement. Eventually, all you are left with is a friendlier version of moralism, in which the gospel is confused with the command to recycle, to vote, to fight poverty, etc.

If you confuse the effects of the gospel with the gospel itself, you will wear out. You will eventually run out of steam and never feel like you have accomplished enough.

In his inaugural address, President John F. Kennedy said, "Ask not what your country can do for you; ask what you can do for your country." For citizens, that is excellent advice. For citizens of God's kingdom, it is backwards: We ask first for what only Christ can do for us, and *then* we are empowered to do good for our country.

Stay centered on the gospel, not social change.

Stay centered on the gospel that brings social change, not the gospel of social change. As individuals, we are constantly tempted to find our primary identity in something other than Christ. Perhaps it's our work, our family background, our nationality, even our church. One of the tests of discipleship is to cling to our identity "in Christ" above all else.

The same is true of churches. We are tempted to find our identity in our worship style, our preaching style, our doctrinal distinctives, our social projects, or our buildings. Church leaders believe that the larger the impact of our ministry, the more legitimate we are as ministers of the gospel. But this kind of affirmation is rooted in outward success, not in our identity as sons and daughters of a loving Father.

Individual Christians can and should be salt and light in their various fields of influence and vocation. We will be involved in public life. Different churches will be involved in various mercy ministries, in caring for the poor, in stewardship of the environment. All churches are commanded to proclaim the gospel. In addition to gospel proclamation, different churches will choose to engage in different avenues of service to the community and for the good of the world.

But we must remember that such activities are the response of the gospel, not the gospel itself. We are united, not by our acts of service, but by our Savior's service even unto the cross. When we seek something other than the kingdom, we become just like any other social agency, except ours is baptized in religious rhetoric. Remember, non-Christians engage in good deeds too. Gospel proclamation makes the difference!

Focus on relieving suffering, both temporal and eternal.

James Emery White tells about attending a conference with leading figures who were considering how best to infiltrate and shape culture for Christ:

> There was much talk of reaching culture, impacting culture, shaping culture—and then it hit me. No one was talking about reaching the people who were making that culture. There was talk of justice and art, but not redemption. In some quarters it is as if we are focusing on the means to the end, only to forget the end. I have noticed this with many new churches planted to "reach the world" and "connect with culture." After sitting through countless such services, the pattern seems the same: enormous effort to connect culturally, great explanations of the practical wisdom and ethic of the Bible, but seldom is given the invitation to actually cross the line of faith in Christ.[3]

White makes a good point. It is easy to seek cultural change apart from the work of evangelism. Of course, it is good and necessary for Christians to engage in acts of mercy. The gospel of God's grace makes us into the kind of people who relieve suffering, both temporal and eternal. But to focus merely on the temporal is to *reduce* the implications of the gospel.

Pastors Steve Timmis and Tim Chester are right: "Social action without proclamation is like a signpost pointing nowhere. Worse still, it is likely to imply either that salvation is synonymous with socioeconomic betterment or that salvation is through good works like those I am doing."[4]

We don't feed the hungry *only* because we want them to know the gospel. But neither do we want our activity of helping the poor *to not* testify to the gospel. In other words, good deeds are done out of genuine love for our neighbor. We do good deeds for *more* than evangelism's sake, but never for *less*. Withholding the gospel announcement from people is to miss our calling. We cannot be satisfied with satisfying physical hunger while never introducing people to the Bread of Life.

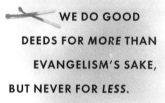

WE DO GOOD DEEDS FOR *MORE* THAN EVANGELISM'S SAKE, BUT NEVER FOR *LESS*.

Social action that relieves temporal suffering is popular right now. It brings the applause of the world. If you tutor inner-city school children, you will receive the world's praise. But once you try to plant a church in the inner city, you may be vilified. People cheer you on when you give people food to relieve their temporal hunger. People jeer when you give the gospel that relieves eternal hunger.

One way to perform deeds of mercy *and* keep a strong emphasis on the weighty matters of the gospel is for preachers to not shy away from the doctrine of hell. D. A. Carson recalls a conversation with a church leader who recommended preaching about hell as a way of keeping the gospel front and center: "As long as you are still preaching the wrath of God against all rebellion and all sin, then you are preserving in your own mind and in the consciousness of believers in the church that you are interested in the relief of suffering both in time and eternity. You start fudging on that corner and you lose that eternal dimension."[5]

Our primary witness is to testify to the power of the gospel, both by our actions (that demonstrate our gospel-changed hearts) and through our words (that urge others to repentance and faith). Our goal is to be good witnesses. Christians are not called to change the world; we're called to testify to the One who has.

Stay confident in the power of the gospel.

If you're a culture warrior, you may think that political machinery is the primary weapon of restoring righteousness to the land. If you're an errand-runner, you might think that grassroots organizations are the way to effect change. If you're an educator, you might think that more programs and government funds will create a better-educated society that will bring about lasting change.

Notice the common thread in each of these approaches: *The gospel needs something more.* The gospel is not enough to change the world. We need to do x, y, and z if we're going to see lasting change. According to this mind-set, power is what brings change, but it's not *gospel* power. We may still believe in the gospel, but we think that something else is the true agent of change in our world.

When you read the New Testament, you can't help but notice that the apostle Paul did not seem very concerned about equipping his churches to address the big challenges facing the Roman Empire in his day. Paul saw himself as a witness to a different kingdom. Jesus hadn't come to overthrow the government; He had ushered in a new kingdom, one that would bring lasting change and (one day) everlasting peace.

In *The Screwtape Letters*, C. S. Lewis writes about the "delicate" position between Christianity and politics. His devilish character, Screwtape, advises a demonic protégé to lead people into either the quietist or the activist counterfeit: "Certainly we do not want men to allow their Christianity to flow over into their political life, for the establishment of anything like a really just society would be a major disaster." This is Screwtape hoping that Christians will embrace the quietist gospel, which seals off the implications of the gospel announcement from the public life of society.

"On the other hand, we do want, and want very much, to make men treat Christianity as a means; preferably, of course, as a means to their own advancement, but, failing that, as a means to anything—even to social justice." Here Screwtape hopes that Christians will fall for the other error, the activist gospel, which trades the agenda of God's kingdom for the agendas of earthly kingdoms. Screwtape elaborates:

> The thing to do is to get a man at first to value social justice as a thing which the Enemy demands, and then work him on to the stage at which he values Christianity because it may produce social justice. For the Enemy will not be used as a convenience. Men or nations who think they can revive the Faith in order to make a good society might just as well think they can use the stairs of Heaven as a short cut to the nearest chemist's shop. Fortunately it is quite easy to coax humans round this little corner.[6]

When a church loses confidence in the simple gospel it proclaims week in and week out, its people become restless and begin to search for whatever they think will give them the power they long for. So we abandon the simple faith of the mustard seed and start climbing the redwood tree. We don't like waiting around for leaven to move through the dough, so we stuff our faces with a ready-made cake. We aren't content with the hidden treasure in the field; we'd rather build a showy palace on the hillside.

Gospel-Driven Activism

We've seen a number of dangers in embracing an activist gospel. Is there any way for us to engage in activism that is driven by the gospel? Yes. While we avoid the activist gospel, we shouldn't avoid gospel-driven activism. Christians are called to be present in the world as salt and light. We have seen good examples of this in the past.

William Wilberforce may be the best example. A British politician and evangelical Christian of the early nineteenth century, Wilberforce played an integral role in the abolition of slavery in England. Early in his career, he realized that he did not have to choose between a spiritual vocation in the church and a secular vocation in society. Instead, he chose to implement the truth of the gospel within the sphere of influence he had been given. The gospel drove his active opposition to the slave trade, but Wilberforce never confused his activism with the gospel itself. He was always concerned to relieve both temporal and eternal suffering. He sought not only to stop slavery here and now but also to save people from eternal slavery to the Evil One.

Another example of gospel-driven activism is the growing adoption movement in evangelical circles. Families are welcoming children from other cultures and races into their homes. They are caring for the fatherless in a way that images the gospel of God's grace incorporating us into His family. We catch a glimpse of the gospel through the actions of these activists.

Prison Fellowship, founded by Charles Colson, is another example of gospel-driven activism. Colson began the ministry not merely to reform prisoners so that they will be good citizens once they are released. He also wanted them to become citizens of God's kingdom. Colson and his team understood that true reform is not behavioral modification, but a change of heart that comes only from the gospel.

The activist gospel is a counterfeit that unites the church around a cause. Gospel-driven activism is the outworking of a church united around the gospel. Avoid the first. Embrace the second.

Scripture Truths

ON THE MISSION OF THE CHURCH: *Matthew 28:18–20; Acts 1:8; John 20:19–23*

ON BEING UNITED BY THE GOSPEL: *Psalm 133; 1 Corinthians 1:10–31; Galatians 2; Colossians 2:6–19; Ephesians 4:1–16; 1 Peter 3:8*

ON THE POWER OF THE GOSPEL: *Romans 1:16–17; 15:18–19; 1 Corinthians 1:18; 4:19–20; 1 Thessalonians 1:5*

The church is not perfect, but woe to the man who finds pleasure in pointing out her imperfections.

– Charles Spurgeon

the churchless gospel

IMAGINE you're from another planet and touring earth. One Sunday you're approaching a place of worship in the midst of a bustling city. The first thing you notice is a colorful sea of parked cars. *Must be popular*, you think. Pilgrims are making their way inside, coming here for an experience that adds value to their life.

The architecture is clearly recognizable. Everyone seems to know where they are headed. Once inside, you notice signs telling you where you are and where to go. Some of the walls have banners and flags. The place is beautiful. You're ready to lose yourself in this space, to forget about what time it is, and to become immersed in the place and the people. The colors reflect earth's autumn season. You see orange and brown, even some hay and cornhusks on display.

In the main hallways, people extend their hands in greeting. Their faces are friendly, and they offer to help you find your way. They shepherd you through this experience. Just before leaving, you reach into your wallet. Finally you say goodbye, exit, and head to your vehicle.

Now . . . stop imagining. Do you know the place I've just described? No . . . not the church. It's the local mall. Think about it. Big parking lot. Recognizable architecture. Directory and signs. Pictures on the wall that seem to say, *You could look like this.* Colorful decorations for the season. Friendly employees. Purchasing something you expect will bring you happiness.

Now wait a minute, you say. *You had me thinking that this was a place of worship you were describing.* Exactly. The mall *is* a place of worship. Just like a football stadium. Just like the halls of academia. Just like a church. In each of these places, we are shaped as worshipers—our affections and desires are formed; our understanding of salvation is molded and shaped.[1]

Churchless Christians?

In recent years, the local church seems to have had less significance to Christians. Some don't understand the importance of the local church existing as an institution. Others belong to a local church and yet don't see the need to attend regularly.

Many pastors react to this lack of commitment to the church by trying to make people feel guilty. The message turns into something like, "You know you should be in church. So just go!" So people come on Sundays, but their response isn't driven by the gospel, and guilt is never the best motivator.

Instead, every Christian should understand that as believers we *are* the church, and that a key function of a church is to gather in worship and then scatter into our respective vocations for the glory of Christ.

The author of Hebrews speaks of the great honor it is to meet together with other believers. And at one point, he warns against "forsaking our own assemblying together" (Hebrews 10:23–25), neglecting to meet with one another for worship. I'm encouraged by a passage like this because it lets us know that the problem of Christians neglecting corporate worship is not new. If the author of Hebrews saw this problem as important enough to address, it must mean that even back in New Testament times, some Christians were neglecting fellowship.

Evangelical Versions of the Churchless Gospel

As evangelicals who emphasize the need for a personal, heartfelt commitment to God, we are often in danger of downplaying the need to be united to a gospel community. There are several versions of the churchless gospel that are making headway in evangelical life. Here are three:

The institutional church is a pagan invention.

A recent book entitled *Pagan Christianity?* attempts to "explore the roots of our church practices."[2] Books that critique the current worship practices of the church come and go. But rarely does a book so vehemently oppose *everything* about the institutional church. The authors are convinced that the house church/organic church movement is the way of the future because it is the only authentic reproduction of the past.

The argument goes like this: For almost two thousand years, the church has been seriously misguided. Layers of tradition have stifled the true Christian experience. In order to recover the early church of the apostles, we must see the church as an organic entity without hierarchy in leadership or religious programs. Christians today should consider abandoning the organized church and adopting home groups or other forms of Christian fellowship without structures that consolidate power.

It is certainly the case that tradition can be damaging to the church. We should be constantly returning to Scripture for justification for our practices. But taking a swipe at all organized forms of church is not the way to seek renewal. Churches are imperfect because people are imperfect, not because of organized hierarchy.

The church is optional for the Christian.

Another way that some Christians fall for this counterfeit is by thinking that the church is just a nice option intended to help you along on your spiritual journey. Perhaps you can find that help elsewhere, like a college ministry or a parachurch organization. You can disciple yourself by finding materials that help individuals study God's Word. Download sermons from your favorite pastor, and you can grow on your own.

I would never demean the good ministry that takes place in parachurch organizations, through podcasts, and through discipleship materials. But all of these ministries are best viewed as an assistance to local churches, not a replacement for them.

The church is a hindrance to true spiritual growth.

Some people believe that the church stifles spiritual growth. They think, *The church is holding me back from my potential.* Unfortunately, church leavers are right to point out that Christians often don't look like Jesus. I'm often befuddled to find people who claim to follow Jesus yet know next to nothing about His life. There are plenty of churches with Christ in their names, but not in their congregations. When the church becomes a place for like-minded people to rally the troops and put on smiles that mask the hidden reality of sin and brokenness, the church can indeed become an obstacle to true spiritual growth for people who love Jesus and want to be formed into His image.

But the solution is not to abandon the church; it's to challenge the church to more Christlikeness. We need to be challenged by Christ's life, His teaching, and the meaning of His death and resurrection. How is it spiritually healthy to leave the church? How does bailing out of the church make us more like Jesus?

Jesus gave His life for the church, His bride. We look forward to the marriage supper of the Lamb. But I'm afraid that some people pit Jesus against the church in an unhelpful way. When it comes to Jesus and His bride, some are rooting for a divorce.

SPOTTING THE COUNTERFEIT
the churchless gospel

STORY	ANNOUNCEMENT	COMMUNITY
The storyline of Scripture focuses on an individual's need for salvation and purpose. The community of faith is at the periphery of this narrative.	The good news is an announcement solely for the redemption of individuals.	The local church is viewed as either an optional aid to personal spirituality, or an obstacle to be discarded in one's pursuit of God.

Why This Counterfeit Is Attractive

There are a number of reasons why Christians, especially evangelicals, find this counterfeit gospel so appealing.

It emphasizes individual spirituality.

We don't want to worship God merely with our lips. We want to worship Him with our lives. We yearn for a personal relationship with God, not the ritualistic religious practices that don't affect life change. Evangelicals believe that we should not merely serve God out of duty, but out of love—out of a changed heart. All of these tendencies are good.

But notice that the focus stays on the individual and what he or she *feels* about God. This tendency can turn on us, and it does. It's also reflective of our culture's fear of boredom or tradition. Every now and then a soloist mangles a song, the sermon doesn't seem to apply to you, or the children's program needs more volunteers. Real life is messy. Retreating to a world where you tailor your spiritual experience for yourself will actually stunt your growth.

It points out the church's faults and challenges us to holiness.

It is good to have an idealistic view of the church. But an ideal can do one of two things: It can either prompt us to work toward the fulfillment of the ideal, or it can paralyze us to the point that we give up. Perhaps our craving for a church full of Christ's presence is God's way of giving us a holy discontent that is meant to stretch our faith and stir our imagination. The faults we see in the church should increase our motivation for seeking the ideal. Denigrating the church because of its shortcomings only undermines the cause of Christ in the world.

Though no local church is perfect, and the universal church often looks more like a cheating spouse than a faithful bride, we are to identify ourselves with this bungling bunch of believers. The church is home. The church is God's beloved. The church has been bought with precious blood. Though the presence of the kingdom is not as intensely felt in the church as we would like, it remains the sign of the kingdom in this age. And if Jesus is content to give His life for an unruly church, we should seek satisfaction in serving His church.

It frees us from having to submit ourselves to outside authority.

The anti-church crowd, especially its popular manifestation in the West, often mirrors our culture's aversion to authority. We don't want to be told what to do. We don't want to submit ourselves or our personal agendas to a body of believers. It is much easier to hop from church to church, feed ourselves online through podcasts or devotional materials, and love people in the abstract, rather than deal with messy situations in our congregation.

Countering the Counterfeit

The churchless gospel is a counterfeit that robs us of the joy of authentic Christian community built upon the announcement of the gospel. How can we listen to the legitimate concerns from critics of the church and yet maintain our commitment to the gospel community? Here are several suggestions:

Let your idealistic view of the church propel your desire for reform.

It is good to question *why* we do things a certain way in worship. We need to be willing to reexamine and even throw out traditions that are unbiblical.

But there is an overly idealistic notion common to the anti-church books. They are built on a premise that says the early church was untainted and uncorrupted by human tradition. The idea is that we need to get back to the early church and things will be better.

To those who want to get back to the early church, I pose this question: *Which early church do you want to be like?*

Corinth? The church took pride in a man's incestuous relationship. Meanwhile, the worship gatherings were not being done decently and in order.

Galatia? Paul was shocked to see that this church so quickly abandoned the gospel.

Thessalonica? This church was grieving in a worldly way, without hope that their loved ones would take part in the coming restoration and resurrection.

Sure, we can learn from the earliest churches. But there is no pristine, untainted, uncorrupted early church that we must aspire to be like.

Those who fall for the churchless gospel may try out an organic option like the house church. But the same idealism that drew them away from institutional churches will be the same idealism that is shattered once they discover the same fallenness, the same abuses of authority, and the same worldliness in these other expressions of church.

The churchless gospel does not lead to church renewal but to ecclesial amputation. More and more disenchanted church members abandon their church families in order to seek the "pure church" of the first century. We keep chasing the pot of gold at the end of the rainbow, only to find it eludes us because it doesn't exist.

Instead of letting our idealism drive us away from the local church, why not let our passion for reform lead us back *toward* the local church?

Let's go back to the gospel of grace. The good news is for people who recognize they are messed up, rebellious, sinful, broken, and dysfunctional. Christianity is for the losers, for the people who recognize their need for salvation outside of themselves. When we fully grasp the nature of our sinfulness, we see that churches are organized groups of these messed-up, broken people who are slowly being changed into the image of Christ through the power of the gospel. Why in the world would we expect the church to always live up to some unattainably high ideal? I'm not saying we shouldn't shoot high. I'm not saying we should be satisfied with Christless churches or gospelless churches. But surely we should give groups of broken people (churches) the same patience we give individual broken people.

THE CHURCHLESS GOSPEL DOES NOT LEAD TO CHURCH RENEWAL BUT TO ECCLESIAL AMPUTATION.

Yes, it's true that Christians are broken, wounded, sinful, and selfish. It's also true that, too often, this sinfulness will be visible in our churches. But that's why we need each other. We need to challenge one another to purity, to discipline one another, to encourage one another, to love one another within the structures

Christ has ordained. Just as we need Jesus in us as individuals to slowly remake us into His image, we need Jesus-filled people in churches if there is any hope for the church to reflect the glory of Christ to the world.

Love people despite their faults (that is how Christ has loved you).

How can you best demonstrate to the world the forgiveness of God given to you in Christ Jesus? By granting that forgiveness to those within your church.

In one memorable *Peanuts* comic, Linus yells, "I love mankind . . . it's people I can't stand!" G.K. Chesterton said something similar: "I learned with little labor the way to love my fellow-man and hate my next-door neighbor."

Truth be told, we talk about loving others, but we're quick to hit the road when loving people gets hard. Pastor Kevin DeYoung is right: "The ideal of community can prevent you from loving your real community. Those most in love with the idea of community are most likely to be impatient with real community."[3] We're not called to love an idea; we're called to love our brothers and sisters in Christ.

C. FitzSimons Allison believes that those who reject institutional Christianity may be flirting with docetic tendencies. Docetism was the ancient heresy that said Christ only appeared to have a body when He was actually just a spiritual being. Allison writes:

> "I'm religious but I don't believe in institutional Christianity" is often another Docetic way to say, "I want to be spiritual without any of the ambiguities, frustrations and responsibilities that embody spiritual commitment." I want to be a parent, but I don't want to change a diaper. I want to be on the soccer team, but I want to do my own thing over in the corner, show up for practice

whenever I feel like it and do whatever I please.

Institutions are embodiments and substantiations of ideals, aims, and values. Docetism is a special abnegation of any responsibility to incarnate ideals, values, or love. It is altogether too easy to love and care in the abstract. Concrete situations of diapers, debts, divorce, or listening to and being with someone in depression and despair, is the test of real love. Docetism is the religious way to escape having love tested in the flesh. All of us are tempted to audit life rather than to participate fully and be tested by it.[4]

If Christ remains committed to us—as broken and messed up as we are—why would we not remain committed to His followers? Why would we bolt out the door when our church experience becomes a hassle? What looks more like Jesus, to hit the road or to stay with a congregation through good and bad?

Too many people think that the church's problems are an obstacle to becoming more like Jesus. Actually, the opposite is true: Commitment to bear with the church's problems is the method by which we become more like Christ. Dietrich Bonhoeffer was right: "Those who love their dream of a Christian community more than the Christian community itself become destroyers of that Christian community even though their personal intentions may be ever so honest, earnest, and sacrificial."[5]

In the end, I don't want to divorce Jesus from His bride. I want to see Christ's bride become more like Christ. Just as the facial expressions and physical characteristics of two lovers begin to reflect one another after many years of companionship, I want to look more like Jesus. For all of us, that won't happen unless we stay committed to His people, challenging and encouraging others as they challenge and encourage us.

Let the church's common confession of hope shape you.
Cyprian of Carthage famously said, "You cannot have God for
your Father unless you have the church for your Mother." The
Reformers echoed this statement. I think it's accurate, as long
as it's qualified. If we're talking about salvation, I don't want to
give the church too much credit. The Holy Spirit births us into
the kingdom; the church is the instrument, the ambassador that declares the
gospel. But the quote is right if it means
that loving God as your Father will lead
to submission to the church's motherly
oversight. In that sense, I say yes.

> CHURCH SHAPES
> US . . . AND OUR
> FAMILIES IN WAYS WE
> WOULD NEVER IMAGINE.

   The statement does points out the
anomaly of an unchurched Christian. You don't find such a person in the New Testament. Christians belong to local churches,
which gather together and affirm each other's profession of faith
in Christ. It is this confession of hope that shapes us as a people.

   Church shapes us. Gathering every Sunday is a habit that reminds us who we are. It strengthens our belief in Jesus. Living according to a calendar that says, "Every Sunday is for the Lord,"
shapes us and our families in ways we would never imagine.

   Think about the different calendars that are provided in our
world. Those who work in retail know that there is a shopping
calendar. Halloween. Thanksgiving. Christmas. Valentine's Day.
Easter. Mother's Day. Father's Day. July 4 and other summer sales.
Retailers know which calendar events bring in big bucks. Shop-
pers often orient their purchases around those days.

   Take the sports calendar. Pro football in the fall, every Sunday
afternoon and Monday night, leading up to the Super Bowl. Then
you've got basketball, baseball, and maybe even soccer. From
preseason games to the championship games, there's a timetable
that we can orient our life around.

   Broadcast television provides another calendar. You watch

certain shows on certain nights, at certain times of the year. Your days of the week can be oriented around which television shows come on which night.

None of these calendars is bad in and of itself. We participate in other calendars all the time. Kids have a school calendar. Your work load probably has peaks and valleys. We go on vacations in the summer.

But what is the heart of the church's calendar? Every Sunday morning is a mini-Easter. Every Sunday morning we orient our life around the truth that Jesus Christ is Lord, and God raised Him from the dead. That calendar is formative. We reorient our life every week by centering ourselves on that truth and by gathering with the family of God.

Whereas the rest of the world looks at Sunday as the last day of the week, Christians say Sunday is the first day of the week. It's the day Jesus came back from the grave. It's the day we gather to worship the risen Christ. It's the day we show our kids that we belong to the King. We are shaped by our confession, and that confession is expressed in our calendar.

Rituals and traditions shape us and mold us as people. Praying with your children and reading them a Bible story every night is formative of their lives. Deciding to prioritize worship every Sunday—even if that means you miss the ball game or can't go with the travel team, or have to miss a dance recital—tells your kids how important God is in your life.

Consider how many habits in our life are formative. The mall is a multisensory experience that shapes us as people. Look at the signage, often showing images of young attractive models in the latest fashions and accessories. They are telling you, *This isn't you; you need help. Look at what you could be! And if you'll just buy this product, you'll be "saved."*

Think about the worship rituals that takes place in a football stadium. You stand at certain times. You sit at certain times. You sing. Certain foods and beverages are always there. The way that people at a football game respond to the announcer or to the big screen reminds me a little of a liturgical church service where you stand and sit and respond and then have Lord's Supper.

All of these events include rituals and traditions and shape us as people. Traditions and disciplines and habits are powerful. That's why we need to choose them wisely. They form us.

Traditions and disciplines mold us in their image. Visit the mall every week for hours on end, and you will be molded into a consumer. Visit the football field every week for hours on end, and you will be molded into a spectator. Attend church every week to hear the Word of God, and you should be molded into a worshiper of Jesus the King.

Some people object to this kind of emphasis on spiritual discipline by saying, "I don't want to just go through the motions!" You don't say that about brushing your teeth or taking a shower. (At least I hope not!) Isn't it true that *going through the motions* shapes us as people? If your children said, "It's boring in the bathtub. I don't want to wash this week," would you say, "Well, that's okay. I want your heart to be in it"? No, you'd say, "Washing is important; here's why. Now go get in the tub."

I'm not ignoring the place of the heart when it comes to worship. We shouldn't be satisfied by just going through the motions when it comes to church. We don't want to be people who worship God with our lips, but not with our hearts. But we will not become more like Christ by avoiding worship until our hearts become engaged.

Instead, we should join our brothers and sisters, beg God to break our hearts afresh, and ask Him to—through our actions and traditions—shape our hearts into the kind of people He has called us to be.

Look for opportunities to embody the gospel.

The world needs to see the corporate witness to the gospel. You cannot embody the gospel announcement if you are not consistently in covenant fellowship with other believers. You cannot be the Christian you are called to be without being in community. We need each other. We are sent out as missionaries *together*.

We strengthen each other when we're together. Strengthen someone in their walk with Christ, and you are strengthened. You come to give, and in giving, you receive. The more you do for others, the more you grow yourself. "You don't give of yourself to the church. You give *yourself*."[6]

Francis Chan tells a story about a young man who got saved out of the gangs. He was on fire and full of passion. A few weeks later, the guy stopped going to church. When he was asked about his absence, he said, "I had the wrong vision of church. I thought that when I got baptized and joined the church, it was going to be like when I got jumped into the gang. Immediately, we became family. They had my back twenty-four hours a day. If I was sleeping in the street, they were sleeping there with me. We didn't get together just once a week; it was all the time. I guess I just didn't understand church."[7]

At the risk of sounding sacrilegious, I think that former gang member might have better understood what church is supposed to be like than the people in that church. We should be cheering each other on, encouraging one another, and challenging each other to remain on the narrow path. We fulfill God's mission together.

Prepare yourself for the day of judgment.

One reason that we need the gospel community too often goes unmentioned. I need the church in order to be prepared for the day of judgment. It is frightening to think that I would allow myself to be the sole judge of my spiritual condition here on earth. I know how easily I deceive myself. Am I so bold as to say I am the best judge of my spiritual character? No, I need the church to affirm my faith in Christ, to assure me when I doubt, and to lovingly rebuke me when I err. Judgment day is coming!

Have you ever noticed that older people tend be more faithful to church than young people? This isn't true everywhere, of course. But even in multi-generational churches, it's often the older people who are the most faithful.

There may be a variety of reasons for this fact, but I think one reason is clear: people who are older know that the day of the Lord is drawing near. Either Jesus will soon come back, or they will soon go see Jesus. And the closer you get to the end of your life, the more likely a Christian is going to realize the seriousness of walking with Christ.

IF YOU LIVE FOR CHRIST WELL, YOU WILL DIE WITH HIM WELL.

Why is it that so many people showed up at church the Sunday after September 11? Why is it the youth group room fills whenever a young person is killed in a car crash? Because, for a moment, we are shaken out of our slumber. The brevity of life hits us hard. We realize that life is short and that we are not guaranteed tomorrow. If you live for Christ well, you will die with Him well. One aspect of the Christian life is preparation for dying well.

One of the benefits of answering the summons of King Jesus to gather as the church—to be shaped by our confession and our practices, to be strengthened by the Body of Christ—is that it prepares you to be the kind of person who can face death boldly. You are shaped into someone who can deal with death.

So when you begin to experience unusual symptoms and physical limitations—or the doctor sadly informs you that your illness is terminal—you can wipe away your tears. As a Christian you can boldly look death in the eye and say, "You're an enemy of God's good creation. I'll fight you with every fiber of my being. But even if I succumb to the cold clutches of death, I know that you are defeated. Your sting is gone. I will soon be with my Savior, who has conquered you, and even my grave will one day release my glorified body." And it's your fellow church members who will minister to you, comfort you, cry with you, and—eventually—mourn your death and rejoice over your life.

Be willing to submit to spiritual authority.

It is popular today to pick and choose beliefs from various religions. Those who believe that all religions are attempts at grasping the same truth also believe there is no need to submit to any outside authority, such as the Bible or the teachings of a church. You choose to be your own authority, determining your own truth for yourself. In our hyper-individualized, autonomous, anti-authoritarian American culture, the beliefs of the anti-church crowd fit right in with the mainstream.

> GOD'S INTENTION IS THAT WE SUBMIT TO CHRIST... AND CHRIST EXERCISES HIS AUTHORITY THROUGH THE CHURCH.

But my mind is too restless to trust so much in my own ability to pick and choose whatever seems palatable from other religions. I am too conscious of my own defects to argue against the accumulated wisdom of centuries of Christian reflection and adopt a viewpoint that doesn't accord with anyone else. I know my limitations and thus am compelled to trust in the testimony of those who walked and talked with Jesus, and those who have followed Christ for centuries and those who walk with Jesus today.

When we say we believe in Jesus Christ, we are confessing something theologically about who Jesus is. "Christ" is not Jesus' last name. The word "Christ" means "Messiah-King." Next time you are reading through your New Testament, try this. Every time you come across the title, "Jesus Christ," substitute "King" or "Messiah" for Christ. You'll be amazed at how prevalent the idea that Jesus Christ is King is in our Scriptures.

We have a hard time understanding what it's like to live in a kingdom with a king. After all, we elect our representatives. There is no king over us. If you don't like the leader, you change him. If you don't want to participate in the government process at all, you don't have to. No one is even forced to vote.

But as Christians, the kingdom of God is not a democracy. The kingdom of God is about Jesus the King. Just as you would obey an earthly king, you obey the heavenly King. But the Bible doesn't portray this King as a tyrant, lording His authority over us in careless and selfish ways. Not at all. God, in His great love, has graciously allowed us to come into His presence. It should not feel like an obligation to gather with the church body to worship God; it should feel like a privilege. God has called us into His presence, and He has, through Christ's work on the cross, made it possible for us to stand before Him and live. Jesus is the way we approach God, and we can do so with boldness!

We belong to King Jesus, and the King has summoned us. Contrary to what you may think, we do not belong to a church as volunteer participants. We belong to the church because we have responded to a royal summons. The King has summoned us to gather together and hear His Word and fulfill His great commission.

The churchless gospel sidesteps the issue of spiritual authority. Without a church, you take your own discipleship in your hands. But God's intention is that we submit to Christ as our King, and Christ exercises His authority through the church.

The word "church" doesn't refer to a building. The word in Greek is *ecclesia,* and it means an assembly, a gathered community. One of the primary functions of a church is that we gather together. It goes to the very core of who we are as a people. We are a called-out people.

God has called us out of the kingdom of darkness into His

marvelous light. He has called us to be His witnesses. To become a member of a church, you must repent of your sins, trust in Jesus, confess that He is Lord, and then follow Him through baptism. We are the people of God who are called by His name.

A Powerful Display of the Gospel

Our love for our churches is a powerful demonstration of the gospel. It is what gives us our distinctive flavor in a bland world of voluntary associations. Francis Schaeffer points out that Jesus gave the world the right to judge whether we are truly Christian by the way we love one another. "That's pretty frightening. Jesus turns to the world and says, 'I've got something to say to you. On the basis of my authority, I give you a right: you may judge whether or not an individual is a Christian on the basis of the love he shows to all Christians.'"[8]

Allow me to tweak that last line from Schaeffer. It's not how we love *all* Christians that provides the biggest demonstration of our salvation; it's how we love the Christians we rub shoulders with in church, the Christians we bump into on our way to the nursery, the Christians we covenant with when we are baptized, the Christians we break bread with during the Lord's Supper.

It's impossible to demonstrate our love for all Christians everywhere. But the Christians in our local congregation are our family. When we love them as Christ has loved us, we bear the mark of the Christian.

Scripture Truths

ON THE GATHERING OF THE CHURCH: *Matthew 18:15–20; Romans 15:1–7; 1 Corinthians 11:17–33; 14:26; Hebrews 10:19–25*

ON THE CHURCH AS CHRIST'S BODY: *Romans 12:4–8; 1 Corinthians 12:12–27; Ephesians 1:20–23; Colossians 1:18*

ON THE "ONE ANOTHERS": *John 13:14, 34–35; 15:12, 17; Romans 12:10; 15:14; Galatians 5:13; Ephesians 4:2, 32; 5:19, 21; Philippians 2:3; Colossians 3:13; 16; 1 Thessalonians 4:18; Hebrews 3:13; James 5:16; 1 Peter 3:8; 4:9; 2 John 5*

ON SANCTIFICATION: *John 14:15; 2 Corinthians 3:18; 5:17; Romans 6:4; 8:13; 12:1; 13:4, 12–14; Galatians 5:16–17; Colossians 3:8–10; Philippians 1:6; 2:12–13; 1 Peter 1:15–16; 1 John 3:2*

the counterfeit gospels

COUNTERFEIT	STORY	ANNOUNCEMENT	COMMUNITY
THERAPEUTIC	The Fall is seen as the failure of humans to reach our potential. Sin is primarily about us, as it robs us of our sense of fullness.	Christ's death proves our inherent worth as human beings and gives us the power to reach our full potential.	The church helps us along in our quest for personal happiness and vocational fulfillment.
JUDGMENTLESS	Restoration is more about God's goodness than his judgment of evil or his response to rebellious humanity.	Jesus' death is more about defeating humanity's enemies (death, sin, Satan) than the need for God's wrath to be averted by His sacrifice.	The boundaries between the church and the world are blurred in a way that makes personal evangelism less urgent and unnecessary.
MORALISTIC	Our sinful condition is seen as the individual sins we commit. Redemption comes through the exercise of willpower with God's help.	The good news is spiritual instruction about what we can do to win God's favor and blessing upon our earthly endeavors.	The church is a place where people who believe like us can affirm each other in keeping the standards of the community.
QUIETIST	The Grand Narrative of Scripture is personal and applicable primarily to those areas of life that we define as spiritual.	Christ's death and resurrection is a private and personal message that changes individual hearts. It is not concerned with society and politics.	The church focuses on self-preservation, maintaining its distinctiveness by resisting the urge to engage prophetically with culture.
ACTIVIST	The kingdom is advanced through the efforts of Christians to build a just society. We are the answer to our prayers for a better world.	The gospel's power is demonstrated through political, social, and cultural transformation brought about by involved Christians.	The church finds its greatest unity around political causes or social projects.
CHURCHLESS	The storyline of Scripture focuses on an individual's need for salvation and purpose. The community of faith is at the periphery of this narrative.	The good news is an announcement solely for the redemption of individuals.	The local church is viewed as either an optional aid to personal spirituality, or an obstacle to be discarded in one's pursuit of God.

epilogue

witnesses of the gospel

The gospel is good news. It is a word to be proclaimed.
You cannot be committed to the gospel without being committed
to proclaiming the gospel.

– Tim Chester and Steve Timmis

A GOSPEL that does not lead to mission is no gospel at all, for the biblical gospel reveals the heart of our missionary God. But how can we best proclaim the gospel in a world that is simultaneously hungry for good news and turned off by many of the truths of Christianity? How can we be faithful witnesses to the gospel?

We have seen that the gospel is a three-legged stool. The gospel story provides the context for the gospel announcement, which then births the gospel community. Many of the common methods of evangelism focus on one leg of the stool to the exclusion of the other two. But the best way to witness to the gospel is to incorporate each of these three aspects.

Tell the Gospel Story

James Emery White, pastor and former president of Gordon Conwell Theological Seminary, tells a story of an Episcopalian priest speaking to some parents who visited him with a notepad filled with questions from their teenage son. One of his questions was: "What is that guy doing hanging up there on the plus sign?"[1]

In the past, many Americans had a cursory knowledge of the Christian faith. Those who did not attend church or adopt the religious beliefs of their Christian neighbors knew which church they were *not* going to and which religion they were rejecting: Christianity.

Today our country is rapidly changing. We can no longer assume that people instinctively feel the need to be in church or have a relationship with God. When we proclaim the gospel, we cannot assume that our friends have a cohesive, cultural understanding of Christianity. Christendom is disappearing.

When I was in seminary, I worked part-time as a tutor helping children who were having a difficult time in school. I began engaging one of the families with the truth of the gospel. They told me that they had seen *The Passion of the Christ* and had been moved to tears, but they didn't know why they found the film so powerful. So they asked me to come over one day and go through the entire Bible with them in an hour. What an exercise! How do you share the gospel with a family that has no concept of the truths at the heart of Christianity?

You do what Jesus did on the road to Emmaus. He helped his disciples understand how all of history revolved around His death and resurrection (see Luke 24:15–27). When our friends and family members express interest in Christianity, we need to be able to tell them more than a five-point outline. We must know the gospel well enough to be able to answer questions they may ask.

In previous generations, tools like "the Four Spiritual Laws" and the Evangelism Explosion program dominated the field of personal evangelism. These tools have been effective for many people, and we can be grateful that the Lord continues to use these methods. But now that our society has moved in a direction that is increasingly post-Christian, these methods have begun to show their age. Why? They focus on the gospel announcement without providing the context of the gospel story.

Traditional evangelistic strategies are not necessarily deficient in what they say, but in what they *assume*. These methods assume that the lost person already has some basic Bible knowledge. But without a religious framework in which the character of God is largely understood and the nature of sin is acknowledged, such presentations make little sense. Unfortunately, we now live in a world in which few people understand these truths.

Even the gospel presentation known as the Romans Road is deficient if not set within the larger context of *creation, fall, redemption,* and *restoration.* The presentation usually begins with Romans 3:23 (*All have sinned and fall short of the glory of God*), before moving on to sin's penalty (6:23), God's intervention (5:8), and our response (10:9–10, 13). I've used it on many occasions—it is Scripture, after all! Surely one can't argue against the Bible as a gospel presentation!

But the problem with the Romans Road is that it doesn't begin at the beginning—it doesn't begin with God. *Even Romans doesn't begin with Romans 3:23.* In Romans 1, Paul speaks of the character of God and the devastation of human rebellion. Romans 2 indicts all of us—Jew and Gentile alike. Romans 3 underscores the depravity of human nature.

In other words, even the Romans Road (at least as it is popularly used) makes sense only within an overarching narrative that is scriptural. The presentation assumes that people know who God is, what God demands, who we are, what our problem is, and how God has acted in history to bring restoration.

The deficiency of the Romans Road approach is not the verses of Scripture, but the disappearance of the framework in which these verses make sense. When the people around us no longer hold to a biblical framework from which to make sense of these truths, the Romans Road turns into a series of cobbled-together propositions that are disconnected from the story of Scripture.

My suggestion? When presenting the gospel, tell the story. Follow the contours of the Bible's storyline. Don't be afraid to connect the dots for people. Sometimes, non-Christians will remember certain Bible stories (the family I mentioned earlier remembered Noah's Ark), but they don't know how they are connected to the Bible's storyline or how they point to Christ.

There are some great resources available that aid us in telling the story. Two children's books are especially helpful, *The Big Picture Story Bible* (Crossway) and *The Jesus Storybook Bible* (Zondervan).[2] I've given away these books, and one of my motivations is that the parents, through reading to their kids, will learn the gospel story too!

Other resources that are helpful in this regard are books like *According to Plan* by Graeme Goldsworthy and *God's Big Picture* by Vaughan Roberts (both published by InterVarsity Press). The Story is a web and print-based tract (see www.spreadtruth.com). that explains the gospel message in terms of four key questions: How did it all begin? (Creation.) What went wrong? (Fall.) Can anything be done? (Rescue.) What will the future hold? (Restoration.) The answers point to God's creation and mankind's fall, and God's rescue and restoration.

Use whatever tract, evangelistic presentation, or resource that best suits you and the person with whom you are sharing the gospel. Just make sure that you outline the basics of the gospel story.

Make the Gospel Announcement

It is possible to so focus on the cosmic sweep of the Bible's story of redemption that we fail to make the gospel announcement and call sinners to cross the line from unbelief to belief. We forget to make the story of good news for the world the story of good news for individual sinners who must accept the work of Christ on their behalf.

The gospel announcement is absolutely essential to presenting the good news. But how can we make the gospel announcement in a way that is faithful to Scripture?

I suggest we begin with the Gospels. At its most basic, fundamental level, making the gospel announcement is telling the story of Jesus. If you are meeting with someone over a period of several weeks, perhaps you should go through *Christianity Explored* and read through the Gospel of Mark.[3] Or maybe you will choose to read Matthew, Luke, or John together.

If you only have a short amount of time, give an overview of the gospel story—creation, fall, redemption, and restoration— and then make the gospel announcement by following the contours of the story of Jesus. Talk about His identity as God, His virgin birth, His temptation, His miracles, His teaching, and His ministry. Just talk about Jesus! If you're worried that you won't get every theological nuance right in your presentation, just open one of the Gospels and walk a person through it.

Don't forget what you are doing as you share the gospel: You are calling someone to repent and trust in Jesus, to follow Christ the rest of their life. Does it not seem premature to call someone to follow a Jesus he or she knows next to nothing about? Jesus is not merely a means to an end, such as "heaven," "a purposeful life," or "peace through trials." Jesus *is* the end. We are not calling

> JUST TALK ABOUT JESUS! . . . JUST OPEN ONE OF THE GOSPELS AND WALK A PERSON THROUGH IT.

people to make a quick decision to settle their eternity. We are calling them to *trust, love, and follow* this Jesus as their King. It is paramount that they know the Jesus they are being called to follow, and the best way to introduce people to Jesus is by taking them to the Gospels.

Once you've introduced someone to Jesus, you make the gospel announcement: "This Messiah-King was crucified for your sins, was raised from the dead, and is Lord of the world." Explain the death of Christ and how it applies to us; explain the significance of the resurrection; explain what it means to submit to Jesus as King.

The gospel announcement, when properly made, will lead to a call for response. Our work is not finished if we simply tell the story of Jesus and never call people to repent of sin and put their trust in Christ's work on the cross for our behalf. Even though it's important to use wisdom in discerning when and how to call for repentance and faith, *we must urge people to cross the line.* At some point, a person needs to realize that they are not part of God's kingdom and that they can and must cross the threshold into God's kingdom by repenting of their sin and trusting in Christ alone for their salvation.

Invite People into the Gospel Community

Many people equate sharing the gospel with inviting people to church or to an activity with a Christian group, since after all, people should hear the gospel in church, right? "What's important is not that we proclaim the gospel with our lips, but that we proclaim it with our lives," they say. "Why not let our lifestyle be our evangelism?"

Other push back against such talk. "The gospel is a verbal proclamation. You must speak the gospel. Your lifestyle isn't evangelism; it only backs up your evangelism. Inviting someone to church isn't sharing the gospel!"

Let me tread carefully into this debate. First, it should be said that the gospel announcement is made, in most cases, verbally. We speak the truth of the gospel with words. There are only two God-ordained ways of proclaiming the gospel with our actions: baptism and the Lord's Supper. These are the only two signs. There is a statement erroneously attributed to Francis of Assisi: "Preach the gospel always; when necessary use words." Yet Francis took the Great Commission ("preach the gospel to all creation" Mark 16) so literally that he preached to the birds and animals too! So I agree with those who say that lifestyle evangelism, by itself, is inadequate.

On the other hand, there is something powerful about inviting people to witness the gospel community in action. The "lifestyle evangelism" crowd makes an important point: we don't witness to the gospel apart from who we are as witnesses. Our witness to the gospel with words is backed up by how we live out the implications of the gospel with our actions.

TWO GOD-ORDAINED WAYS [PROCLAIM] THE GOSPEL WITH OUR ACTIONS: BAPTISM AND THE LORD'S SUPPER.

Though I disagree with sloppy statements that make our actions on par with preaching the gospel with our words, I believe that the "lifestyle" and "church-focused" evangelistic strategies have rightly reminded us of the power of Christian community as an embodied presentation of the gospel.

So here is what I recommend: *Tell the gospel story. Make the gospel announcement. Invite people into the gospel community.* When you are sharing the gospel with someone, go ahead and invite them to your church. Let them see how the church worships. Open up your home and your life to people, and let them see how church members minister to one another, pray for one another, challenge and encourage one another. The church should be a living apologetic of the gospel we proclaim.

Some pastors today promote the idea of "belonging before believing." If by "belonging" we mean welcoming people who attend church before they believe in Christ, I'm all for it. But I fear that much talk of "belonging before believing" actually downplays the urgency of believing in Christ. It is counterproductive to treat people as if they were Christians (giving them access to the Lord's Supper, letting them serve on various mission trips, etc.) before they have placed saving faith in Christ. Regardless of the good intentions behind this shift in mind-set, churches that say this may be minimizing the importance of crossing the threshold of faith.

Welcome people to your church service. Let them see the gospel community on full display. But keep the boundary lines between belief and unbelief, saved and lost, church attendee and church member clear and distinct. These distinctions aid us in our witness to the world and keep people from confusion regarding who the people of God are.

Story, Announcement, Community

The gospel is a story to be entered, an announcement to be proclaimed, and it births a community to be experienced. I pray this book will not be seen as the last word on the gospel or on the counterfeits that vie for our devotion, but that it will be a helpful addition to the ongoing reflection on the gospel and its power to change our lives. May the God who has acted so graciously on our behalf fill us with his grace as we spread his gospel to a lost world!

notes

Introduction: Counterfeit Gospels Versus the Greatest News of All

1. Jefferson Davis, President of the Confederacy to the Confederate Congress, August 18, 1862, quoted by John K. Cooley in *Currency Wars: How Forged Money is the New Weapon of Mass Destruction* (New York: Skyhorse, 2008), 113.

2. Quoted in John Cooley, 127.

Chapter 1: The Gospel Story

1. Ben Patterson, *God's Prayer Book: The Power and Pleasure of Praying the Psalms* (Grand Rapids: SaltRiver, 2008), 193.

2. C. S. Lewis, *The Weight of Glory* (New York: HarperOne, 1980), 32–33.

3. Fyodor Dostoevsky, *The Brothers Karamazov* (New York: Farrar, Straus and Giroux, 1990), 235-6. It should be noted that Dostoevsky puts these words in the mouth of Ivan, the atheist brother, who remains determined *not* to believe this message of restoration, no matter how good it sounds.

4. Herman Bavinck, quoted in Albert Wolters, *Creation Regained* (Grand Rapids: Eerdmans, 2005), 11.

5. C. S. Lewis, *The Last Battle* (New York: Collier/Macmillan, 1977), 183–84.

Chapter 2: The Therapeutic Gospel

1. Lucille Ball, *Love Lucy* (New York: Putnam Adult, 1996), 244.

2. Charles Spurgeon, as retold by Tim Keller, *The Prodigal God* (New York: Dutton, 2008), 60–62.

3. *National Post*, "Reality Bites", July 21, 2008.

4. The Gospel of Thomas, Saying 107, trans. Marvin Meyer, *The Gospel of Thomas: The Hidden Sayings of Jesus* (New York: Harper Collins, 1992), 61.

Chapter 3: The Judgmentless Gospel

1. Alexandyr Solzhenitsyn, *The Gulag Archipelago 1918–1956* (New York: Harper Perennial, 2002).

2. The history of this film is told by Dan Auiler in *Vertigo: The Making of a Hitchcock Classic* (New York: St. Martin's Griffin, 2000).

3. C. S. Lewis, *The Problem of Pain* (New York: Harper Collins, 1996), 130.

4. See Michael Horton, "Whatever Happened to Sin?"; Westminister Seminary, 2007 at http://www.wscal.edu/faculty/wscwritings/horton.osteen/whathappenedtosin.php.

5. Os Guinness, *Unspeakable* (New York: HarperOne, 2006), 217.

6. Timothy Stoner, *The God Who Smokes: Scandalous Meditations on the Faith* (Colorado Springs: NavPress, 2008), 97–98.

7. Greg Gilbert, *What is the Gospel?* (Wheaton, Ill.: Crossway, 2010), 44.

8. N. T. Wright, *Evil and the Justice of God* (Downers Grove, Ill.: InterVarsity, 2006), 178.

9. Dinesh D'Souza, *Life after Death* (Washington, D.C.: Regnery, 2009), 185–200.

10. Miroslav Volf, *Exclusion and Embrace* (Nashville: Abingdon, 1996), 303.

11. Milton Mayer, *They Thought They Were Free* (Chicago: Univ. of Chicago, 1955), 184–85.

Chapter 4: The Gospel Announcement

1. Graeme Goldsworthy, *According to Plan: The Unfolding Revelation of God in the Bible* (Downers Grove, Ill.: InterVarsity, 1991), 73.

2. Graeme Goldsworthy, *Gospel-Centered Hermeneutics* (Downers Grove, Ill.: InterVarsity, 2007), 58-59.

3. Ibid., 59.

4. C. S. Lewis, *The Chronicles of Narnia* (New York: HarperCollins, 2001).

5. Kate DiCamillo, *The Tale of Despereaux* (New York: Scholastic, 2006).

6. Martin Luther, quoted by John Stott in *The Cross of Christ* (Downers Grove, Ill.: InterVarsity, 1986), 216.

7. Roger R. Nicole, "Postscript on Penal Substitution" in *The Glory of the Atonement* (ed. Charles E. Hill and Frank A. James III (Downers Grove, Ill.: InterVarsity, 2004).

8. John R. W. Stott, *The Cross of Christ* (Downers Grove, Ill.: InterVarsity, 1986), 224.

9. N. T. Wright, *The Resurrection of the Son of God* (Minneapolis: Augsburg Fortress, 2003), 266.

10. Adrian Warnock, *Raised with Christ* (Wheaton, Ill.: Crossway, 2010), 124.

11. N. T. Wright, *Surprised By Hope* (New York: HarperCollins, 2008), 67.

12. G. K. Chesterton, *The Everlasting Man* (Redford, Va.: Wilder, 2008), 192.

13. G. E. Ladd, *The Gospel of the Kingdom* (Grand Rapids: Eerdmans, 1959), 128.

14. I have written about the practical implications of subverting Caesar's lordship in *Holy Subversion* (Wheaton, Ill.: Crossway, 2010).

15. *Martin Luther's Basic Theological Writings,* ed. Timothy Lull and William R. Russell (Minneapolis: Fortress Press), 94.

Chapter 5: The Moralistic Gospel

1. Mark Galli, *Jesus Mean and Wild* (Grand Rapids: Baker, 2006), 112.

2. Mary Eberstadt, "Is Food the New Sex?" in *Policy Review* #153. http://www.hoover.org/publications/policy-review/article/5542.

3. Tim Keller, *The Reason for God: Belief in an Age of Skepticism* (New York: Dutton Adult, 2008), 180.

4. Ibid, 177.

5. As quoted in Justin Taylor, "Imperatives–Indicatives=Impossibilities," 3 May 2010 blog at http://thegospelcoalition.org/blogs/justintaylor/2010/05/03/imperatives-indicatives-impossibilities/.

6. As Quoted in Philip Yancey, *What's So Amazing About Grace?* (Grand Rapids: Zondervan, 2002), 45.

7. Victor Hugo, *Les Miserables: A New Translation by Julie Rose* (New York: Random House, 2008), 90.

8. Ibid, 96–97.

Chapter 6: The Quietist Gospel

1. Erwin W.Lutzer, *Hitler's Cross* (Chicago: Moody, 1998), 100.

2. Mark Galli, "Defeating the Conspiracy," *Christian History*, issue 62.

3. "He Lives," words and music by Alfred H. Ackley. Copyright 1933, renewed 1961, The Rodeheaver Co.

4. Dionysus, quoted in Rodney Stark, *The Rise of Christianity* (Princeton, N.J.: Princeton Univ. Press, 1996), 82.

5. Bill Wallace's story is told by Daniel Akin in *Five Who Changed the World* (Wake Forest, N.C.: Southeastern Baptist Theological Seminary, 2008).

6. Charles Spurgeon, Sermon No. 1300, June 18, 1876 at the Metropolitan Tabernacle, Newington; as quoted in Christian Buckley and Ryan Dobson, *Humanitarian Jesus* (Chicago: Moody, 2010), 21.

7. Dietrich Bonhoeffer, quoted by John R. W. Stott in *The Message of the Sermon on the Mount* (Downers Grove: InterVarsity Press, 1978), 62

8. D. A. Carson, *Christ and Culture Revisited* (Grand Rapids: Eerdmans, 2008), 228.

9. Lesslie Newbigin, *Truth to Tell* (Grand Rapids: Eerdmans, 1991), 73.

10. Eberhard Bethge, *Dietrich Bonhoeffer* (New York: Harper & Row, 1970), 228.

11. Tullian Tchividjian, *Surprised By Grace: God's Relentless Pursuit of Rebels* (Wheaton: Crossway, 2010), 134-5.

12. Newbigin, *Truth to Tell*, 52.

Chapter 7: The Gospel Community

1. Gina Welch, *In the Land of Believers* (New York: Metropolitan Books, 2010), 152.

2. Ibid, 187–8.

3. Joshua Harris, *Dug Down Deep* (Colorado Springs: Multnomah, 2010), 200.

4. Tim Chester and Steve Timmis, *Total Church* (Wheaton, Ill.: Crossway, 2008), 50.

5. J. I. Packer, *Concise Theology: A Guide to Historic Christian Beliefs* (Carol Stream, Ill.: Tyndale, 2001), 194.

6. Mark Dever's address "The Church Is the Gospel Made Visible," Together for the Gospel conference, 15 April 2010, Louisville, Kentucky.

7. Scot McKnight makes this point in *A Community Called Atonement* (Abingdon: 2007), 86.

8. John Stott, *The Living Church* (Downers Grove, Ill.: InterVarsity, 2007), 32.

9. Joseph Hellerman, *When the Church Was a Family* (Nashville: B&H Group, 2009), 132.

10. Jesus speaks of heaven as the Father's house with many rooms in John 14. The Greek indicates that this is a rest stop for weary travelers on their way to a greater destination.

11. Catherine Claire Larson, *As We Forgive: Stories of Reconciliation from Rwanda* (Grand Rapids: Zondervan, 2009), 213–14.

12. Chris Armstrong, *Patron Saints for Postmoderns* (Downers Grove, Ill.: Inter-Varsity, 2009), 123.

13. Dietrich Bonhoeffer, *Life Together* (New York: HarperOne, 1978), 34.

Chapter 8: The Activist Gospel

1. Russell Moore, "You Are Not Your Worldview," chapel message at Southern Baptist Theological Seminary, 4 March 2010.

2. Amy Sullivan, "Young Evangelicals: Expanding Their Mission" http://www.time.com/time/nation/article/0,8599,1992463-3,00.html.

3. James Emery White, *Christ Among the Dragons* (Downers Grove, Ill.: InterVarsity, 2010), 97.

4. Tim Chester and Steve Timmis, *Total Church* (Wheaton, Ill.: Crossway, 2008), 78.

5. D. A. Carson, "Proclaiming the Gospel and Performing Deeds of Mercy" found at http://thegospelcoalition.org/resources/a/Proclaiming-the-Gospel-and-Performing-Deeds-of-Mercy.

6. C. S. Lewis, *The Screwtape Letters* (New York: Harper Collins, 2001), 126–27.

Chapter 9: The Churchless Gospel

1. This point is made at the beginning of James K. A. Smith, *Desiring the Kingdom* (Grand Rapids: Baker, 2009).

2. Frank Viola and George Barna, *Pagan Christianity? Exploring the Roots of Our Church Practices* (Carol Stream, Ill.: Tyndale, 2008).

3. Kevin DeYoung, "The Church" at the NEXT 2010 conference, 29 May 2010, sponsored by Joshua Harris and Sovereign Grace Ministries.

4. C. FitzSimons Allison, *The Cruelty of Heresy* (Harrisburg, Pa.: Morehouse, 1993), 37–38.

5. Dietrich Bonhoeffer, *Life Together* (New York, HarperOne), 36.

6. Jonathan Leeman, *The Church and the Surprising Offense of God's Love* (Wheaton, Ill.: Crossway, 2010), 129.

7. Francis Chan, "A Gathering Force" (Catalyst Space: http://www.catalystspace.com/content/read/article_francis_chan/).

8. Francis Schaeffer, *The Mark of the Christian* (Wheaton, Ill.: Crossway, 1976), 161.

Epilogue: Witnesses of the Gospel

1. James Emery White, *Christ Among the Dragons* (Downers Grove, Ill.: InterVarsity, 2010), 86.

2. David R. Helm and Gail Schoonmaker, *The Big Picture Story Bible* (Wheaton, Ill. Crossway, 2004); and Sally Lloyd-Jones, *The Jesus Storybook Bible* (Grand Rapids: Zondervan, 2007).

3. Rico Tice and Barry Cooper, *Christianity Explored* (New Malden, Surrey, UK: Good News Company, 2005). Available at Amazon.com.

acknowledgments

IN 2009 alone, for the first time in human history, over one million books were published. As I think about how many books are available, I am filled with gratitude that you, the reader, have chosen to read this particular book at this particular time. So, first of all, I thank you for your time, and I pray that you will find this book to be a reliable guide in thinking through matters "of first importance."

I am most grateful to my wife, Corina, for the way in which she has encouraged and supported me during this project. I thank my parents and grandparents for the Christian heritage they have given me, and Corina's parents for their unceasing prayers for our family. I'm grateful for my brothers, Justin and Weston, and my sister, Tiffany, for all our table conversations about these matters. Our discussions have sharpened my thinking.

I am thankful for Ken Polk and Kevin Minchey, two pastors in particular under whom I have had the privilege to hear the biblical gospel proclaimed clearly and consistently. I am grateful for the pastors, scholars, and authors who took the time to read and recommend this work. Special thanks to Matt Chandler for writing the foreword and for embodying the gospel in the way he and his church have journeyed through trials together.

Many friends have offered constructive criticism and helpful suggestions: Phillip Bethancourt, Michael Bird, Chris Brauns, Darryl Dash, Kevin DeYoung, Mark Galli, J. D. Greear, Owen Strachan, Bobby Jamieson, Jonathan Leeman, Scott Long, Tony Merida, Eric Peterson, and Ken and Carrie Saxton. I'm also grateful for Madison Trammel for having the initial idea for this book and for his editorial guidance through the writing process. Thanks also to Dave DeWit, acquiring editor at Moody Publishers, as well as developmental editors Chris Reese and Jim Vincent for their enthusiasm for this project and their helpful insights.

THE GOOD NEWS
WE ALMOST FORGOT

In *The Good News We Almost Forgot* Kevin DeYoung explores the Heidelberg Catechism and writes 52 brief chapters on what it has shown him. The Heidelberg is largely a commentary on the Apostle's Creed, the Ten Commandments, and the Lord's Prayer and the book deals with man's guilt, God's grace, and believers' gratitude. The result is a clear-headed, warm-hearted exploration of the faith, simple enough for young believers and deep enough for mature believers.

MOODY
PUBLISHERS

moodypublishers.com

Reverberation

Reverberation explains the pulpit ministry and traces the theme of how the Word continues through the life of the church. Both theological and practical, *Reverberation* focuses on how the church hears, responds, discusses, implements and is transformed by the Word. No high-octane production, superstar personalities, or postmodern entreaties, just stuff that is really good and really powerful!

moodypublishers.com